Obscurist Occulto
Hiding from the Definition of Meaning

Further Zen Ramblings from the Internet

Scott Shaw

Buddha Rose Publications

Obscurist Occulto:
Hiding from the Definition of Meaning
Copyright © 2020 by Scott Shaw
www.scottshaw.com
ALL RIGHTS RESERVED

Cover Photographs by Scott Shaw
Copyright © 2020—All Rights Reserved

Rear Cover Photograph of Scott Shaw
by Hae Won Shin
Copyright © 2020—All Rights Reserved

First Edition 2020

This book contains material protected under International and Federal Copyright Laws and Treaties. Any unauthorized reprint or use of this material is prohibited. No part of this book may be reproduced or transmitted in any form or by any means, electronic or mechanical, including photocopying, recording, or by any information storage and retrieval system without express written permission from the author or publisher.

ISBN 10: 1-949251-32-2
ISBN 13: 978-1-949251-32-6

Library of Congress: 2020946272

10 9 8 7 6 5 4 3 2 1
Printed in the United States of America

Obscurist Occulto
Hiding from the Definition of Meaning

Introduction

Here it is, *The Scott Shaw Zen Blog 17.0*, originally presented on the *World Wide Web*. All of the writings presented in this book were written between May and September of 2020.

As was the case with the previously published volumes based upon *The Scott Shaw Zen Blog;* entitled: *Scribbles on the Restroom Wall*, *The Chronicles: Zen Ramblings from the Internet*, *Words in the Wind, Zen Mind Life Thoughts, The Zen of Life, Lies and Aberrant Reality, Apostrophe Zen, The Abstract Arsenal of Zen and the Psychology of Being, Zen and Again: The Metaphysical Philosophy of Psychology, Tempest in a Teapot and the Den of Zen, Buddha in the Looking Glass, Wo Ton' of the Blue Vision, Zen and the Psychology of the Spiritual Something, Pyrophoric Zen, Fragments of Paradox, Zen: Traversing the Entity of Non-Entity, Zen and the Ambient Echo: The Psychological Philosophy of Being*, and *Paritical Zen and the Life Science of Becoming No Thing* this volume is presented exactly as it was viewed on *scottshaw.com* with no rewriting, punctuation, or typo corrections. From this, we hope you will receive the original reading experience.

This volume of internet ramblings is presented with the date and time listed as to when each blog was originally posted. Also, the blogs in this volume are presented from last to first. With this, we hope to present a transcendence back through time as opposed to an evolving evolution. In addition, we left out the traditional *Table of Contents* in an attempt to leave this volume with a much more free-flowing reading experience.

Okay, there's the information and the definitions. Read on… We hope you enjoy it. And, be sure to stayed tuned for the ongoing *Scott Shaw Zen Blog @ scottshaw.com.*

Your Words Have No Meaning
13/Sep/2020 12:08 PM

When you hear a language from a different land do you understand it? The answer is that you probably do not. So, the question becomes, because you do not understand what that other person is saying, do their words have any meaning? The answer would most probably be, yes they do, but they do not have any meaning to you. Then, one can ask, if those words do not have any meaning to you do they possess any meaning to your ultimate reality? The answer would be, no.

Have you ever attempted to communicate with a person who does not speak your native language? You are speaking words to that person but because they do not understand your language they have no idea what you are talking about. Thus, do your words have any meaning to that individual? Based on the reality of that person, do you words have any meaning at all? The answer would be, no.

Have you ever said something to someone and they appeared to understanding what you were attempting to explain? But then, sometime later, you heard from some other individual that they were told what you had spoken to that original person but what they said you said was completely misinterpreted? What was explained about what you said was completely wrong. If people quote you wrongly do your words actually have any meaning?

Have you ever written something, hoping to convey a particular ideology or a specific set of information, but then someone else took a word you wrote here, a sentence you wrote there, turned them around and presented a completely fabricated presentation about what you were actually attempting to articulate? If people do not quote you fairly, truthfully, or completely, and hope to use your own words to falsely depict your true philosophy, do your written words actually have any meaning?

In life, we all hope to communicate what we believe we know and how we think we feel. We want others to understand what we are experiencing and how we encounter and interpret life. But, as all words are so open to interpretation, do they actually have any meaning?

Have you ever taken the words someone else has written or spoken and altered them to place your own spin on how you would like that person to be viewed by others? If you have, not only have you done a disservice to that person but you have shown your own true colors as a human being or lack thereof as you have decided that you hold the key to be the true interpretation of what that individual actually hoped to convey. In religion we see this all the time. People are constantly interpreting holy scriptures. In the world of academia, we constantly find this, as well. Academics always debate the validity of a person's philosophy or their literary or artistic advancement and/or contributions. But, the interpretation of what one has said or written is wholly limited by the mental mind frame and intellectual abilities of the individual doing the interpretation. Thus, anything anyone says about something someone else has organically proclaimed must first be viewed through the lens of that individual's own biases. In any others words, whatever anyone else says about what someone has spoken or written is false by its very regurgitation. Again, does someone's words actually possess and meaning?

Life is defined by your interpretation of what you see, read, and hear. What you say and write is interpreted by the inner-mind definition of anyone who hears or reads it. Thus, the one thing you can be sure of, though we all may hope it to be another way, is that your words have no meaning—at least they have no true and absolute meaning to anyone but yourself as you are the only one who holds the key to their true interpretation.

The Meditation of Letting Go
12/Sep/2020 07:44 AM

When you wake up in the morning what is the first thing that you think about? For most, they wake to thinking about what they are planning to do during the upcoming day. Maybe they wake up full of desire, (of one form or another). Maybe they have emotion dominated feelings. Most people, from the moment they wake up, fill their mind full of thoughts and this process goes on all day long until they finally fall asleep at night. But, is this the best way to live life? Is this the best way to create your mind?

In the Eastern tradition of spirituality there is the understanding of Sādhanā or spiritual practice. This is when someone consciously guides themselves towards the spiritual realms of reality with the hopes of forming themselves into a more conscious individual.

In the practice of Sādhanā one traditionally wakes at Brahmamuhurtha, *"The time of Brahma."* Which, depending on the tradition, is at either 4:30 AM or about an hour and a half before sunrise. Once one wakes up they wash themselves and then they sit for meditation. Though this is a formalized spiritual tradition that has been passed down for thousands of years, it to is a, *"Doing."* But, any, *"Doing,"* is a, *"Thing,"* that hold the mind bound.

The fact of the matter is, most people do not try to make themselves mentally any better. They do not attempt to guide their mind towards a deeper understanding of Self and reality. They just Do. Their whole life they have been taught to Do, so they just Do. Even if they walk the Spiritual Path, as all they know is Doing, that is all they Do. But, true meditation is not defined by the, *"Doing,"* it is defined by the, *"Undoing."*

What is meditation? Meditation is letting go of the thoughts in your mind. The reason so many people find it so hard to meditate is that all they know is thinking. Thus, taking control over the mind is nearly impossible. Yes, pranayama techniques such as Nadi Shuddhi can be helpful in calming the mind. But, a calmed mind is not necessarily a meditative mind.

So, what is the answer if someone wishes to truly meditate during Brahmamuhurtha or otherwise? The answer is to let go.

Here's a simple meditation technique that you can employee to easily guide your mind towards true meditation at any time you desire. I call it, *"The meditation of letting go."* And, that is the basic technique that you employee, just let go.

Sit down, close your eyes. See the darkness that your consciousness now embraces. Certainly, there will be various thoughts roaming around your mind. Let them go. Don't fight them. Don't try to control them. Simply let them go.

Whatever is in your mind, do not justify it, do not rationalize it, just let it go.

If you are like most people, various ideas and thoughts will come to your mind any time you sit for meditation. Maybe there is a person or a situation in your mind. Let it go. Maybe you are upset with someone or something. Let it go. Maybe you are happy, enthralled, or in love with someone. Let it go.

The mind controls all of us. What we think about on a constant basis comes to be the definition of our life. It comes to guide our life.

Most people never attempt to take any control over the control their mind has over them. Those who do commonly attempt to fight the mind. But, all that does—all any of that does is to cause a case of constant disharmony. The cure; let go.

The letting go meditation is very easy to perform. There is no grand formalized technique that you must be initiated into. Just let go. Anytime anything formalizes in your mind, just let it go.

Wherever you are, whatever you are doing, close your eyes and let go. By doing this, you can enter into a state of profound meditative grace. All you have to do is let go.

*   *   *

12/Sep/2020 07:42 AM

If you don't know that you have a disease do you actually have a disease?

White Balance
11/Sep/2020 10:15 AM

For anyone who has ever filmed a movie on a professional level they understand the concept of White Balance. This is the same for people who shoot for television or other means of formalized distribution.

For those of you who may not know, White Balance is the method of balancing your color temperature. White Balance is where you set your camera's lens to shoot at a constant and perfect state of color. The reason you do this is so that unrealistic colors do not cloud your image.

The way you gain White Balance is to focus your camera on a pure white object. This object can really be anything: a bounce card, a white handkerchief, whatever… As long as it is pure white.

Various cameras have various ways to adjust White Balance. As the video and the digital age came upon most video cameras have an auto White Balance setting. But, this auto function is oftentimes far less than perfect. So, the true professional always sets their White Balance manually.

The thing is, you can't just set your White Balance once and let it ride through your entire day of filming. With each lighting change, the White Balance changes so you need to reset it for every alteration of light; be that natural light or artificial light.

Once upon a time, it was very-very important that your White Balance was right on if you hoped to get your movie distributed. Every time an independent film was presented to a distributor they would check things like resolution and White

Balance. If your White Balance was off, your film may be rejected.

Something happened somewhere around the early 1990s, however. Altered visual styles began to become accepted in the mainstream. I think to television series such as *CSI Miami* where I am sure they filmed their scenes with perfect White Balance but they altered the visual image to posses a very obvious orange hue in post.

The thing about White Balance and its importance is, if your original image is not perfect it is very difficult for it to be altered with any sense of color precision. It is for this reason that following White Balance protocols is essential in the creation of any filmed footage if you want it to be able to be presented with color perfection.

In the recent decades the home movie craze has taken hold. Think about how many people broadcast visual images filmed via the camera on their computer, their DSLR camera, or even their phone. As these technologies have taken hold, the acceptance of what is or is not acceptable has changed radically. Think about how many movies are now filmed on a person iPhone. Combine this with all the visual effects that are readily available and the landscape of independent filmmaking has profoundly changed.

Though the world has changed and what is or is not visually acceptable has evolved, there still remains a level of excellence that must be possessed by any film or visual project if you hope to reach the mainstream. Think of any A-market movie you see. Think of any TV show you watch. Though some do things like say, *CSI Miami* did, and alter their image in post production, what they film is done so with an established understanding of accepted standards and protocols.

What does this tell us? What it tells us is that, yes, you can do whatever you want in the realms of abstract, artistic filmmaking. But, the standards that exist have not left us. If you hope to move your project from only being viewed on people's computers and/or their phones you really need to gain the understanding and put into practice the protocols of such things as White Balance if you hope to move your film(s) into the world of the mainstream.

*   *   *

11/Sep/2020 09:06 AM

When you don't have a strong foundation of positivity in your life you look for a reason to become angry.

The Goodness Directive
10/Sep/2020 11:44 AM

Assignment for the Day:

Do something good today.

Do something positive that helps someone.

Say something nice about someone—maybe somebody you don't even like.

Say something nice to someone. Compliment them.

Give someone a gift.

If you find yourself thinking negative thoughts or find yourself about to say something negative or mean; catch yourself. Turn it around and say something nice.

Take today and do something nice, good, and positive.

You can do this everyday if you want. That's a great way to live your life. But, if nothing else, start with today.

Make this a day that you base in goodness, doing something good, saying nice things, giving, and making everyone's life just a little bit more positive.

Make today a day of positivity.

The Secrets That You Keep
10/Sep/2020 09:18 AM

Think about something that only you know. Something that you never told anyone.

We all have that certain something. Something that is locked only in our mind. Something that we have kept to ourselves. Something that we lived and, for whatever reason, we never communicated to anyone else.

Think about that thing. Isolate it in your mind. Why did you never tell anyone?

For each of us, there is an individualized reason why we have kept that certain something a secret known only to ourselves. In some cases it is shame. In other cases it is fear. For some, it may be that they believe they will be harshly judged if the truth is known. There are also those individuals, of a higher calling, that keep that secret based upon an altruistic mindset of not wanting someone else's life to be hurt or damaged if the truth was revealed. Whatever the case, we each hold a secret. For some, they hold many.

Some people claim that all of a person's secrets should be revealed. In many cults, (some that claim to be a religion), that is how they maintain control over their flock. They find out a person's secrets and then they hold them over their head.

From a psychological perspective, some professionals claim that a person must release all of their secrets to truly be free. I know I used to go to this shrink and she suggested that I expose all of my hidden life secrets to family members. I wrote a letter to one of my family members hoping to free myself of a mental burden. But, I was always sorry I did that. It did nothing for the betterment of me. It made me feel no better. As it didn't change anything, (how could it?), all it did was diminish how I felt about myself in the image I projected and how that other person interpreted my life.

And, that's the thing—that's the reason why we all hold things inside; we believe that by telling someone that certain secret we will never be viewed the same again—we will never be viewed the way we hoped to be viewed. And, for the most part, that is the truth. Revealing is always very revealing. The fact of the matter is, most people don't want to know your inner secrets. They do not have the mental aptitude to process that information in a caring, understating, and enlightened manner.

Some people live in denial. That is never a good a thing. They hide what they did from themselves. They refute their life happenings. That's not healthy. But, the truth be told, sometime keeping the deep dark inner secret, that only you know to yourself, is the best way to transverse through life in a manner that allows you to maintain a strong self image and to have other people see you as something more than a victim or an iniquitous individual.

Love, Anger, Samadhi: Your Mind Can Produce Anything It Wants to Produce
09/Sep/2020 03:51 PM

How do you feel?

What do you feel?

When you are feeling something, are your feelings controlling you or are you controlling your feelings?

Have you ever tried controlling your feeling?

Most people spend their life being controlled by their feelings. When they are feeling whatever it is they are feeling, that feeling holds control over them.

Think about a time when you were very angry. Were you controlling that feeling or was that feeling controlling you?

Forget about defining why you were angry. The fact was, you were angry. That feeling dominated your existence. It made you feel a certain way. It made you do certain things. Perhaps, that feeling of anger made you do something very bad that hurt someone else. Why did you do that thing that hurt someone else? Answer: Because you were angry and that feeling took control over you.

Think about a time when you were in love. Though certainly not as devastatingly overpowering as the feeling of anger, it is certain that when you were feeling it, that feeling of love took over your entire being.

You had met someone. For whatever reason, they touched that spot of love in you. That feeling took over your entire being. It was all encompassing. Perhaps it made you act a certain way. Perhaps it made you do a certain thing. Whatever the case, whatever you did was motivated by that feeling of love.

When you feel anger, do you ever step back from that emotion? Do you ever take control over your feeling and tell yourself to stop feeling anger? Do you possess that power over your emotions or do your emotions have total control over you?

You do have that power if you choose to exercise it. Why don't you exercise it?

Have you ever decided to make yourself be in love? Have you ever decided to feel love for the person who is next to you? Whether you truly love them or not is unimportant. Whether they naturally instigate that feeling of love inside of you is not the question. If you decide to, you can cause yourself to experience that true sensation of love for anyone you want. You simply need to do it.

Me, I do it all the time. It feels great.

For those few people out there who are actually seeking samadhi or enlightenment, they are most commonly telling themselves that they can never reach that pinnacle. That they are not pure or holy or meditatively practiced enough to experience that emancipation of inner knowledge. Some have even turned to drugs and believed that the false experience(s) that those chemicals provide are a glimpse into true nirvana. But, anything that is evoked by external chemicals is solely a creation of that chemical; whatever that chemical may be. If it is not organic, than it is not real.

This being said, enlightenment is obtainable. Let go and know. Let go of all of those predetermined emotional and thought out barriers that you have planted into the pathway of your mind and simply let satori arrive. You can create it. It is already inside of you. If you allow yourself to be enlightened you are enlightened.

People allow their feelings to control them. They allow their emotions to dominate what they think. They allow their feelings to control what they do. From this, their emotions come to be the defining factor for their life; either in a negative or a positive fashion.

But, you can be in control of all of that. All you have to do is be in control.

Your mind can produce anything it wants to. But, for you to truly be the master of your existence you must take control over your mind.

Feelings feel great. Some, like anger or jealously, feel horrible. Other, like love make everything better.

You know what they feel like. You know what they do to your mind and your life. You can be in control of all of your emotions. You just have to choose to be in control.

Next time you are angry, stop it! Control it! Shift your frame of reference.

Next time you are sitting next to someone, love them. Just let the feeling rise in you.

Next time your mind is turned towards cosmic awareness, allow enlightenment to be what you are.

Everything is possible. It is all in your mind. Be in control of your mind and life becomes such a much more interesting landscape of experience.

A Movie Within a Movie Within a Movie
09/Sep/2020 09:53 AM

A little while back someone showed me a review of one of my films where the reviewer says something like, *"Scott Shaw's films are like fever dreams…"* …I really need to have the book published where I had a bunch of the reviews of my films collected. Some of them are very creative and/or funny.

A movie within a movie within a movie… That's a hype line that Donald G. Jackson and I came up with when were completing, *Guns of El Chupacabra.* We realized that we had created a movie with multi levels of storylines converging into one climatic ending. …We knew what we were doing when we were creating that film. We knew we were creating several story situations that could each have become movies on their own. But, we also knew that we were not going to do that—we were creating one film with multilayers allowing the viewer to witness settings and circumstances from many different perspectives.

This multilayered film presentation is something I have continued forward in actualizing in many of my later narrative films.

I get it… Some people don't understand why I would do that. But, for me—from my *Zen Filmmaking* perspective, like I say over and over again, *"The stories have all been told."* What I hope to do is to create, like that reviewer suggested, *"A fever dream."* …Something—a film that steps beyond the traditional story-driven, seen it all before, mumbo-jumbo. I want it to be abstract. That is what my filmmaking is all about! That is what I am all about!

Think about your life. How many things are going on at one time? How many different things are going on in your life in any given moment? I am sure if you were to break them down and separate them into isolated elements they would each be very different. Each person you interacted with, each thing that you do; they are all very different—very varying elements. Yet, you are the common factor in all of that. You are living a movie within a movie within a movie. A movie the climaxes in your brain with your interpretation of all of those isolated happenstances.

Life runs in a million different directions all the time. The more things you are involved with, the more people you know, the more things that you do, the more complex and multilayered your life becomes. Sure, we can get all Zen here and say simplifying makes all things more spiritual and pure. But, life is life is life, we do and we want to do. Thus, the more we do the more levels of life we encounter. All life is a movie within a movie within a movie… It is all how you decide to decipher that concoction that makes you who you are—that defines how your life movie is going to unfold and how it will be interpreted.

Some people will get what you are doing. They will especially get you if what you do falls under the definition of, *"Normal."* Step beyond the normal, step into the realms of art, however, and few will understand your reasoning. That does not mean that they are right and you are wrong. It only means that you live in the world where it takes an artist to comprehend the presentation of your life.

*   *   *
08/Sep/2020 12:30 PM

How long does a mistake remain a mistake if you do not correct what you have done?

How long does a lie remain a lie if you do not tell the truth?

The Pathology of Gore
08/Sep/2020 09:28 AM

Think about the people who enjoy movies that involve gore. Think about the people who like to watch movies where people are hurt, tortured, brutalized, or killed. Think about the people who enjoy watching movies where the good person is taken to task and blamed for the bad actions of someone else. What is the motivation for watching a movie like that?

Maybe you are one of those people who enjoy watching movies like that. Do you ever ask yourself why you desire to view movies where people are hurt or killed?

There are a lot of movies made on the lower budget realm of the spectrum where this genre is embraced. There are also some higher budget projects that embrace this category of film. But, in any of these cases, why are these type of films even made? What benefit do they provide to the greater good?

Some people I have spoken with, who like this brand of filmmaking, claim, *"That's how life really is."* But, is it? I don't think so. Sure, there is a lot of bad behavior in the world—there are a lot of people who do hurtful things, but, for the most part, people are not out there literally running other people through a meat grinder.

Most actors are prostitutes. They will do any role they are offered as long as they are paid. This is the same with film crews. But, at the source point of any of these films (of any film) is someone who envisions them—someone who creates the story idea. Why do they create stories with this theme? Why do they wish to create a movie where people are hurt? What do they get out of it? What does the world receive from it?

Have you ever taken a look at the life of a person who is into gore? Have you ever studied the mind of a person who is into gore? Where is their life in the larger spectrum of reality? Are they living at the higher end of finances and mental awakening?

Personally, I do not like anything that glorifies hurtful negativity on film or anywhere. I do not find any joy in watching someone get hurt, in any manner, even if it simply fantasy on the screen. Whenever I am somehow forced or tricked into watching something that leads to gore or to meaningless dismemberment or just abuse, in any manner, it makes me very upset. I believe that is the hoped for response from these films. That is what the filmmakers wants the audience to feel. But, is negativity, pain, hurt, or damage ever a good thing? Do you like in when you are hurt?

Sure, some people relish in witnessing or creating pain in others. But again, look at their life. Where are they on the spectrum of existence?

All of life begins with what you choose to do. Some people claim that what they do is simply, *"Who they are."* But, that is an excuse. You can be in control of what you think and what you do if you choose to be in control of what you think and what you do. Remember, if what you think and what you do and what you enjoy watching on the screen is the embodiment of pain and suffering; hurt or damage, all you are doing is allowing that mindset to take control over your thoughts and the thoughts leading to the actions of others.

Embrace goodness, rebuke badness on all levels and the world becomes a much better place.

* * *

07/Sep/2020 12:44 PM

When was the last time that you did something nice, good, or helpful for someone and didn't let them know that you did it?

* * *

06/Sep/2020 07:19 AM

Can you judge a person by their past mistakes?

Everything That You Want
05/Sep/2020 10:37 AM

Pretty much everybody has a desire about what they want from and out of life. Though these desires certainly change over time, think how much of your life has been based upon desiring and attempting to obtain what you want.

If these things are small, and not all that expensive, then they are pretty easy to obtain. But, then there is that entire other spectrum of those things Out There that cost big money, require other people's approval, and are, at best, only a hoped for dream.

"That person got it, why can't I?" Particularly in the film industry, this is a statement I've heard so many times. But, you are not that somebody else. You are you. Moreover, how much of what you see is reality? How much of what you believe something to be, actually is that thing?

For example, think of that most beautiful and physically perfect form a person you saw and you just knew that you could be in love with. You see them. Maybe you even meet them, but, for most, you never get to know who they truly are. Thus, you are only left to the fantasy of what could have been forever. But, a fantasy is only just that; a fantasy. It is never a reality.

I feel blessed in that there has been a few times in my life where I saw and met that girl who just took my breath away. We walked down the relationship road but we hit a snag. The girl was not who or what I thought she would be. In a couple of these cases we had a great time together, for a moment or two, but she just was not the true person for me. So, the relationship ended.

For anybody who has been in one of those situations, I believe you will agree. What you see on the surface is rarely the person that is on the inside. They have their quirks, they have their flaws, they have their inadequacies, they have their psychological glitches, (just like we all do), and from that, what you hoped would be, could never truly be.

Me, I have been suffering from intense migrates my whole life. I have been left with chronic anxiety disorder and not a too small amount of psychological malfunctioning due to having experienced one of those really messed up childhoods that you never really get over. My body's shot and in pain from martial art and motorcycle injuries. But, you don't see that on the outside. How could you? How could anyone? And, this is the thing, what is seen is not what is unseen. You can never see the unseen, you can never anticipate the unseen. But, if you choose to seek out that desire, you may be forced to confront, and maybe even live with, what is not seen.

When people are young they have this belief that they will obtain all of their desires. When they fall in love, they believe, it will conquer all. But, all anyone has to do is to look to the life of anyone— look at how many unfulfilled lives there are and how many relationships have fallen apart. All of these people had a desire. In some cases their desire was met, in some small or large way, but then it evaporated and what were they left with? Only the No More.

So, what does this tells about life and desires? What does it tell us about us seeking our desires? The main thing I believe it tells us is that life is an illusion. Who you believe that person to be is an illusion—it is only a construct of your own mind. What that thing will give you, if you get it, will change everything for you for the better forever... No. It will simply lead you to new desires.

We are all cast to this life. We are all dealt the cards we are dealt. But, what we choose to desire is what we choose to desire. No one can make us want something that we do not want. No one can tell is our own perimeter of beauty or desirability.

You are you. Though there are a lot of things in life you have no control over, you can take control over what you see and believe is desirable. And, if you desire something, you possess the ability to not fall under the illusion of that something, believing that it will be that Perfect Thing that will bring all that you want in life to your doorstep.

People are who they are. That is all they will ever be. Things are what they are. They get old and break. Life situations are always dominated by a million levels of circumstance(s) that you can never anticipate. So, know that you will never know—know that you can never be guaranteed that Any Thing or Any Person will actually bring grand perfection into your life. Know this and then you can watch any desire that enters your mind blow away like a leave in the wind.

Please
04/Sep/2020 09:03 AM

"Please," I've opened the door, you go in first.
"Please," It's a crowded subway, take my seat.
"Please," Can I have what you are offering?
"Please," May I have some more?
"Please," May I borrow that item from you?
"Please," Don't do that.
"Please," Do that.
"Please…" You are so full of shit.

Please is one of those words that sets the standards for a high level of communication. It immediately defines the nature of a conversation and the actions that are to follow.

Please is one of those words that should be used all of the time but so rarely is.

Take a look at your own life. Take a look at your own communications. How often do you use the word, *"Please?"* How often do you put the concept of, *"Please,"* into action before you do something?

Do you use the world, *"Please,"* or do you simply take what you want and/or do what you do without ever thinking about the other person.

The concept of, *"Please,"* is a defining factor for the life of everyone. If it is at the forefront of a person's vocabulary, you can be sure that they are thinking and caring about the other person. They are taking their feelings into consideration. If, on the other hand, a person does not use the word, *"Please,"* before they do what they do and simply takes what they want without any care for the impact that taking will create then they are defined by a selfish, uncaring mindset. Who are you? Which one are you?

Take a moment right now and look at the years of your life. Who have you said, *"Please,"* to? Why have you said it? Who should you have said, *"Please,"* to but did not? Why did you not?

Your life/all life is defined and measured via your interactions with other people. Are you a person who thinks about the other person first and says, *"Please,"* or are you a person who simply does what you want, takes what you want, and never even contemplates, *"Please."*

We all leave a wake in our existence. We all leave an impression of ourselves in the minds of others. What we say what we say; we all do what we do. How we behave towards others becomes the ultimate definition of the life we live. What life have you lived? How often do you say, *"Please?"*

Art for Art Sake
04/Sep/2020 07:33 AM

I've forever been a fan of thrift stores. …You never what you are going to find. Most of the time you find nothing. But, every now and then, you find something really cool.

One of the things I used to do in thrift stores was I would take photographs of art that I thought was really bad. I don't what I planned (or plan) to do with those photographs but I just thought that art needed to find its way to eternity. I mean the artist cared enough to drawn or paint it. It meant something to them. But, then it was discarded.

I also used to collect art I found in thrift stores. I guess I still do but to a much lesser degree. I ended up with a lot of paintings. A few, by noted artists, are still on my walls.

I moved about five years ago and I got rid of a lot of it. Commonly, I give the art I have collect away to people who like it—maybe like it more than I. But, back then, when I moved, I gave a lot of it back to thrift stores. And, there was a lot. A treasure trove of art. One piece, I sold on eBay. It was from this primitive artist. The price I got for that painting pretty much paid for all the art I had purchased from thrift stores for the previous decade or so.

As an artist myself, I've painted a lot of stuff over the years. Every now and then I go through it and throw away all the stuff I don't like. I'm told I shouldn't do that. I guess if I had a lot of space maybe I wouldn't. But, I don't. So, I'm damned by the hands of reality.

There've been a few people who've painted portraits of me. I always found that amusing. A couple people have done illustrations and cartoons of me, as well. That's funny too.

Mostly, art is in the eye of the beholder. What one person loves another person sees as horrible.

I remember I went to this retrospective of modern art at this museum a number of years ago. What I saw was that the evolution of modern art was so much like my own artistic evolution. From the simple to the more color intensive and involved. The thing I noticed the most at that retrospective was that the art has all been done. Though each artist may put their own unique twist on their creations, there is no new evolution taking place. It is simply different examples of the same thing.

How much do you think of art? Do you think of art? How much art do you create? Do you create art? Or, are you only a lover or a hater, an admirer or a critic?

Art is everywhere if you see art everywhere. But, do you have the time to see art everywhere? Do you have the mind to see art everywhere? Do you allow yourself to see art everywhere?

Life is beautiful if you see it as beautiful. There is beauty everywhere, even in the things that people do not commonly see as beauty—even in the bad art that you don't like.

Take the time to see the art in everything and everything become a little bit more interesting and everybody becomes a little bit more of an artist.

*　　*　　*

03/Sep/2020 09:19 AM

If you wish to maintain faith in your religion, whatever your religion may be, never expect to receive a payment or a reward simply because you believe.

* * *

03/Sep/2020 07:38 AM

You've just made a big mistake. Now what?

* * *

03/Sep/2020 07:38 AM

Nobody knows anything but everyone says everything.

* * *

03/Sep/2020 07:37 AM

Anybody who creates anything is going to have their detractors.

Who is Holy?
02/Sep/2020 10:02 AM

Who is holy? This is a question I often ponder when I encounter people or hear about people who are walking on the so-called path to higher understanding or god consciousness.

I get it, most people don't care. They veer towards the syndical and when they hear about some religious teacher being defrocked on the news, they believe that is just the way it is. They are all fakes!

This being said, there are also a lot of people who seek a deeper meaning to their lives. But, here is where the problem arises, as these are the people who can be most affected by those claiming to be holy when they are anything but.

Sure, we have all heard of the dastardly things that Catholic priests have done to young children (leave the young people alone!) and the ministers that rave against homosexuality in their sermons and it turns out they too are gay. Not to mention all of the affairs that religious leaders have had and then cry for forgiveness to their congregation so that the money will keep coming in.

But, there is a much deeper situation going on than simply all of that… There are people who truly seek out a teacher. There are people who want to know, to understand, to experience more. These are the people who turn to those who claim to know but this is where the true problem of the dissemination of knowledge arises. Moreover, this is where the true intentions of an individual may be reveled. Why are they teaching? What is their true inner motivation? It is truth or is fame, money, or power?

I think back on an interesting moment in my own life... When I was an undergraduate at the CSUN, I was predominately focused on teaching the martial arts at my studio. But, because I was also involved with the spiritual aspects of yoga, from my youth forward, I was also very involved in expanding on those philosophies. I was offered the opportunity to teach a course on the meditative and spiritual aspects of yoga at the California State University, Northridge Extension College, which I accepted. To make it official, I even used my Sanskrit name. ☺

The interesting thing, at least for me, was that there was also a western man, who had become a Sikh, teaching a course on Kundalini Yoga via the tradition of Yogi Bhajan (Harbhajan Singh Khalsa) at the same time. He instructed his students that they must bring him flowers at the beginning of each class. Some of my students, who were also enrolled in his class, asked if then needed to bring me flowers, as well. I laughing said, *"No."*

For those of you who may not know, the bringing of flowers to one's teacher (one's guru) is very common in Hindu and Sikh culture. But, this was just a White guy. Just someone like me who was trying to spread the understanding. But, unlike me, he proclaimed himself a, *"Spiritual teacher,"* someone who deserved reverence. But, was he? Or, was he just some White guy, dressed up in a turban, riding on his ego?

In any case, I had a very nice young lady in my class. Her boyfriend worked so he could not arrive for the class until later in the evening. But, that was fine with me. All are welcome. The couple asked me on the second class if they could speak with me in private. Sure, I invited them over to my apartment. There, they asked me if I would become their spiritual teacher. I obviously declined the opportunity. My belief is, anybody who believes they are a spiritual teacher is at least lying to the other person but more than likely lying to himself or herself.

I was and am happy to pass on knowledge. I was and am happy to teach a class. But, you don't need to bring me flowers. I'm just a guy… I am not a guru.

By this point in my life I had already had a lot of experience with Eastern (and Western) spiritual teachers who focused on the traditions of the East. I had already seen some who fell from grace due to their iniquitous activates. Others, I had personally experienced not to be operating from a pure space of consciousness. Yet, they all designated themselves to be a, *"Spiritual teacher."* But, were they?

A bit later in my life there was this very famous self-help guru inhabiting the bookshelves and the talk shows. At one point, after my book, *"Essence: The Zen of Everything,"* had been published, I sent him a copy. He replied with a thank you note and a signed copy of one of his books. Great! A year or two later, however, I was in a bookstore and noticed his new book. I opened it up and he had really ripped me and my concept off. I sent him a, *"What's up,"* letter? What I received was a very angry; handwritten, scribbled, fuck you response. …Putting me down and accusing me of all kinds of ego-driven nonsense. What? I thought this guy was supposed to be spiritual? A spiritual, help orientated person would not have written a response like this.

Anyway, I had written a whole essay on this subject many years back and it was up on this website, in association with copies of his two letters. When the man passed away I took it down, however. I am not one of those to speak ill of the dead. During this period of time this man was also accused of a lot of plagiaristic activities and even sued by another author for taking some stuff from his book, etc. But, all that suing stuff, that's not the kind of person I am. People should be nice. They should handle things person-to-person.

I asked then, as I ask now, *"Was that guy a truly spiritual person?" "Was he actually a spiritual teacher?"*

I believe that here arises the problem—the problem that some people simply want to believe. For those of us who care about this kind of stuff, we seek out those who can seemingly provide it. But then, all the bullshit comes into play. All the egos. All the self-proclaimed knowers. Then what? What are you left with when those you listen to turn out to not be spiritual or holy at all?

Obviously, everybody denies the faults and the flaws in their teachers until they are personally confronted with them. That is why worshiping some deity or guru who died years or centuries ago is so easy. You don't have to meet them. You are not forced to encounter their flaws. And, everybody has them. Everybody…

Though some people claim saintliness and godliness, are they? Are they really?

So, here we are left with a choice. …A choice for those of us who seek higher understanding… We must learn from someone but who is worthy of our discipleship?

There are preachers everywhere. There are gurus all over India. There are temples and monasteries all across the globe. But, all that any of us are left with is we, the person, the individual, who seeks to know more. Where do we choose to go? Who do we choose to study from?

Ultimately, there is only us who can know. Enlightenment is not Out There. It is In Here. So, if someone can give you a little guidance, accept it. Take it for what it is worth. But know, each person is only as good as they are. Each person has already fallen from grace. Each person who says anything is only presenting it from their own limited understanding of the subject. Take what you can. Learn what you can. But recognize, it is only you who can translate and transplant any of that Mind Stuff into your own coherent pathway to enlightenment. Never let a teacher become your life. Because ultimately, *"Who spiritual?" "Who is holy?"* My answer, no one.

But What About Those Who Aren't Famous?
01/Sep/2020 12:35 PM

I remember ever since I began attempting to walk down the path of guitar mastery, one of the first things I realized was that the best guitarists I encountered were not famous at all. They never had fans or a big record deal. Yes, I have had the change to meet some very good, very famous guitar players throughout the years of my life, but this same fact remains; the best guitarists I have encountered are completely unknown. So, what about them?

This year, 2020, has seen the passing of some very famous people. I remember back in 2016 there were a lot of deaths of some seminal musicians. The fact is, famous people die all the time. It just brings it closer to home when a seemingly large amount of them die in a close period of time.

Death is always sad. Yes, there are those who walk the path of religion, philosophy, or simply not caring, and they dismiss death as no big deal—an inevitable transition. But, for those who knew a person, those who care about a person, or those who recognize what a person did, death is forever sad and painful.

It seems whenever a famous person passes on; their accolades and their accomplishments are highly reminisced about. That's great! They were one of the few who rose to the top. But, what about the everyone else? What about the person who no one ever heard about? What about the people who did all kinds of good things for all kinds of people, in a small or a large way, but no one ever knew they did it—no one ever cared? What about them?

You know, few of us are ever going to rise to the level of a music superstar or a movie star. Few of us are ever going to be known outside of the people who know us. But, this does not mean that we can't do good things—that we can't make a contribution to the betterment of the everyone and the everything else. It does not mean that we can't do something good that helps others.

So, next time someone passes one, be they famous or not, look to them as the person they were—look to the things that they did. Remember the goodness that they unleashed.

And, for us, the still living, remember life is short. No matter how long we have, it is never enough. So, do all the good that you can. Because good is always better than bad. Even if you are that great guitar player that no one ever heard, that does not mean that you can't do good things for one person, two people, or a whole lot of people. Even if you never get thanked, that does not mean that you didn't do those good things.

Always embrace the good. Always try to help. Always try to do as many good things for as many people as possible for that is the true legacy of a life well spent.

Template for Dharma
31/Aug/2020 10:21 AM

Life is based upon a pattern of actions and reactions. Life is based upon the application of personal choices. Life is based upon your reaction to the actions of others. Life is based upon what you choose to do, how you choose to do it, why you choose to do it, and how what you choose to do affects others.

If you look to life, what one person does has the potential to affect the entire word. A person has a cold. They decide to go into a room with other people. Other people catch that cold. Each of those people then decides to go into rooms where there are other people. In each of those rooms additional people catch that cold. The people who catch that cold then deiced to go somewhere else and others become infected. That cold, initially only impacting the life of one individual, spreads outwards and onwards until the entire world becomes infected.

Did the person who exposed others to the cold they were experiencing think before they acted? Did they consciously contemplate what their cold could mean to other people and to the world as a whole? Did they care what happened to one person, two people, or a million people who were exposed to the cold that they brought to that one gathering? Here lies the essence of life—what one person does to another.

Dharma is the understanding of the universal truth. Dharma is the embracing of the rightness of all things good, true, and righteous. Dharma is one person experiencing the symptoms of virtue and then spreading them outwards to the world not only through their words but also via their actions both consciously undertaken or simply allowed to happen from the rightness of their being.

The problem with dharma is, however, few people feel the inclination to catch the disease. Few people care enough of those outside of themselves to do the things that will positively impact the world; passing on from one person to another to another.

Where do you find yourself in life and what are your life interactions? What obligations do you feel you have towards the world? Do you live in a space of denial? Or, do you live in a space of embracing the dharma while allowing it to spread outwards from yourself?

What is good is obvious. It has always been obvious. There has been no change in what is good throughout time, space, and history. What is bad is also obvious. The difference is, many people relish in badness, for badness, for doing onto others, for making people pay for their undefined crimes, for judging people, for controlling people, makes those who inhabit the lower mind feel empowered and feel good. But, feeling good is not necessarily doing good. In fact, in many cases, it is just the opposite. Good arises from a place of wholly good. It comes from the essence of the goodness of Be-ing.

Where is that true good? It is in all of us. It simply needs to be found, embraced, and emulated.

You can do things that make you feel good. But, that is not the dharma. You can take people to task, because you judge or blame others. But, that is not the dharma. The dharma is the whole sourcepoint of true reality, where what is wholly and truly good exists. It is not based in what your mind thinks. It is not based in what your body does. It is where you allow yourself to step beyond your focus on you and move into the reality where everything is everything, where everyone is everyone, and all that you do emanates from a space of cosmic knowledge; knowing that your every thought, your every action has the potential to affect and to change the entire world.

Helping is Never Hurting
30/Aug/2020 08:42 AM

It seems that I speak a lot about helping and trying to make this world a better place. Particularly, at this point in history, with all the chaos and rioting going on, this concept is constantly front and center in front of all of our eyes.

I get it… Some of you readers out there are probably sick or me bringing up this point; via various methods and words. But, think about it… Isn't helping someone one of the greatest goods? When you needed help, how sad were you when you didn't receive it and/or how happy were you when you did?

Now, at this stage of time and space, many people take to the streets in hopes of changing society. I remember this kind of behavior taking place in the 1960s. Then too, people hoped for change and many people, just as today, instead of having a true game plan, their actions ended up causing damage and hurt to other people.

The thing is, when you are out there in a crowd, when you are a part of the movement, crowd mentality takes over. There's all kinds of adrenalin rushing through your veins, based in frustration and anger. From this, things happen. Things are done to people and to places. Damage is created based in frustration and anger. But, does that help or change anything for the positive? No. At best it hurts someone or something and from this any change that may be enacted is base upon hurt. That is not help. That helps no one or no thing.

This is a very common practice and one of the reason people get the concept of helping totally wrong.

Think about a time when someone you knew was angry with someone. Though that someone did nothing wrong to you, you too may have become angry with them simply because that other person was. This may have caused you to hold ill will towards that person. It may have even caused you to unleash some level of negativity or negative action towards them. But, why? Your actions were based on the emotions of someone else. How did that help? And, who did this hurt?

Did your karma become negativity affected because you did something bad to that someone or that something else? And, did you even think about this? Did you even care?

You know, this is one of things that I find so common in the human psyche. When something negative happens to a person, they always question, *"Why me?"* But, they never look to their past deeds and actions towards others. They never look to their own karma.

The thing is, helping is never hurting. If you believe you are helping someone by hurting someone or something else, you are wrong. You may believe that you are helping that one person but you are hurting someone who will then wish and hope for help. Thus, the cycle of damage is never ending.

I believe we should all take the time to step back from ourselves, think about the other person, and try to help them—try to make their life better. But know, that if you hurt anyone or anything in the process, no matter if that action does help the person you are hoping to help, your actions of hurt will cause you to, at some point, encounter the karma of that hurt. So, if you hurt anyone for any reason, even if you believe you are helping someone else, don't ask, *"Why me,"* when negativity finds you.

    Helping is never hurting.

* * *

29/Aug/2020 07:52 AM

Who did you help yesterday?

Who are you planning to help today?

Don't make excuses, justifications, or rationalizations. Who are you helping and why?

If you only think about yourself, your world becomes limited by your own self-imposed selfishness.

Help!

Bigger Than Their Own Mind
27/Aug/2020 10:50 AM

You know when you are saying something that is not right. You know when you are doing something that is wrong. You have a mind and you have conscience but do you use them and do you allow them to guide your life? Some people do. Some people don't. But, all that occurs to a life that does not embrace the illuminated mind is a life set to constant conflict, emotional turmoil, and dissatisfaction.

There is the Sanskrit term, *"Prabhāsvara-citta."* This term refers to the illuminated mind. It describes a mental place where the individual lets go of demeaning individual desires, wrong thinking, and wrong actions that then allows them to enter into a state of refined consciousness where true goodness and illumination can be found.

Do you ever think about refining your mind? Do you ever think about refining your actions in the world so that others are not impacted by what you say or do? Do you ever consciously control your words and your action? Do you ever step back from all of the nonsense that is going on around you, driving you to be guided by random emotions, so that you can actually take control over your mind, which will then direct your action down the road to higher consciousness?

Currently, we find ourselves at a place in history where there is a lot of societal upheaval. There are riots taking place in the streets here in the United States and across the globe. People, motivated by the actions of those in power, desire change. From this, many have taken to the streets in protest—protests that have almost universally led to violence, looting, and a generalized upheaval.

Most people, motivated by emotion, do what they do with little thought of how what they do will affect the great whole. They want what they want, based upon what they what. This is obviously a very selfish form of consciousness, however. It is based upon one person desiring something for themselves but claiming it is for something more. It is one person hurting another, stealing from another, blaming others for what they are doing when what they are doing has little sense of care for the people they are impacting.

The thing that most people are not realizing is that there is a lot of victim mentality going on right now. What is taking place right now in history is motivated by victim mentality.

Think about it… Why are these ongoing protests taking place? Why are new ones forming just when the previous ones were becoming quiet? Why? Because someone else was hurt. Thus, the protestors have a new reason to rebel. But, is this rebellion coming from a pure space of consciousness or is based on undefined reactive emotion? If it were coming from a pure space of consciousness, there would not be people looting, damaging property, and hurting other individuals. There would not be people attacking the police. That is war. That is not conscious protest.

Certainly, we can all understand that people have been hurt by the powers that be in this world. Certainly, we may not like what is taking place by the edicts evoked by certain businesses that treat certain clients in a demeaning manner. But, how a person reacts sets the stage for what happens next.

For example, I think back to a time many years ago. I walked into a pawnshop as I saw a vintage guitar that I truly planned to buy if it was not damaged. I asked the old man behind the counter if I could see it.

To elaborate… Back then, there were a lot of people who did not like men with long hair. It wasn't that I was not dressed nicely; I was. But, all he saw was my long hair.

His reaction to me… He rudely said, *"I not here to entertain you."* I couldn't believe what he just said. I was a serious customer. Though it went back and forth for a few minutes, he wouldn't let me touch the guitar. He lost a sale over his prejudice and this was long before Yelp or other ways to file a business complaint. …It was long before people cared about the customer like the blowback that occurred when people were asked to leave Starbucks.

There were times before this when restaurants would not serve my friends and I simply because we had long hair. Cops had accosted me simply because of my appearance. In my youth, I have been jacked, had to fight so many times, I have been stabbed, and even shot in my leg all because I was white. So, you see this kind of stuff can happen to everyone/anyone. But, it is all how you react to those actions that set the stage for your life and your further emancipation.

I think if we look at much of the turmoil that is taking place at this point in history, it is based upon people's dissatisfaction with where they find themselves in life. But, what is that dissatisfaction based upon? How much of what a person is feeling is created by themselves? Why are they embracing victim consciousness? And, are people simply looking for a means to react? Are they simply looking for something to give them a reason to become angry?

The fact is, most people on this planet are not on the road to enlightenment. They are not thinking about the greater good, the higher self, or the betterment of all. All they are thinking about is getting what they want. If they have it, they are happy. If they do not, they are angry. If people treat them the way they want, all is well with the world. If not, look out; it's time for hurting and looting, all presented under the guise of protest.

I am not diminishing the pain that certain people and certain races may feel. What I am saying is that all the world begins and ends with you. So, what are you doing about you to make you a better person? What are you doing to bring yourself to a higher state of consciousness?

Let's be clear, anger-based protesting does not do that. All that does is allow you to be control by the, *"Out There:"* be that people, political parties, the powers that be, or the person who throws a brick at you simply because they do not like your job or the color of your skin.

Now, I understand, for the most part, the people who read this blog are not the ones out there causing damage to the life and the livelihoods of others. But, even if you're not throwing brinks at the cops and breaking out store windows so you can steal what's inside, that does not mean that you are not causing damage to the life of other people and to the world as a whole. Be clear, if you hurt one person you hurt everyone.

Take a moment... Think about the people you have hurt and ponder the larger life space you have damaged. How much time do you spend thinking about this kind of thing verses how much time you think about what someone has done to you? When you hurt that person, when you did that thing, were you thinking about enlightenment? Were you pondering higher consciousness? Were you in control of your mind and your life actions as opposed to allowing your emotions and your desires to dominate what you did and why you did it?

This is where all of the damage that incites these riots begins. It begins with one person doing one thing.

There is also a different place where one can exist. Illumination and enlightenment and general world betterment come from a place of refined consciousness. They come from a space of controlling your own mind and, thus, controlling your actions.

You may not care about enlightenment. Few people do. But, you care about the way you feel, don't you? You care about the way other people treat you? But, if you are not the source point of making you a better you, if you are not at the crux of becoming better, if you are simply reacting to the emotions of all of those things controlled by all of those people Out There, how can you be in control of anything? At best, it may make you feel emotionally just a little bit better for a moment or two if you scream your lungs out. But, that leads to nothing. That makes nothing any better.

The pathway to better always begins with you. It begins with what you focus upon. It begins with you making the choice to guide your mind towards a better, deeper understanding of not only you but generalized reality, as well. You do not become better by throwing a brick. You do not become better by saying something mean or doing something that you know (or don't care) is wrong. You only become better when you choose to rise above what you think and what you feel and move towards a space where you, and what you think and feel, is not the only thing that matters.

If all you do is look at life Out There, you will always be controlled by the Out There. If you based all that you do upon what you think about the people and the goings-on Out There, you will always be dominated by the Out There. Out There is always out there. You can never truly control it.

If you actually care—if you actually care about the Out There and those who dwell Out There the only way you can be sure to make anything any better is to begin with you. If you are better, if you do nothing to hurt or damage, then the world has become that much better—that one person better. This is where true change takes place, when you are bigger than your own mind and you seek true goodness via not being dominated by what you think, what you feel, what others are telling you what you should think and feel, and instead embrace illumination.

Illumination is the light. It is the inner light within you. It's there. It's not hard to find. But, you must choose to seek it out.

Take a moment. Forget the Out There. Look inside. Find the light. Let everything become better.

What Do You Like?
25/Aug/2020 07:40 PM

For each of us, from time to time, we find ourselves in a space of dissatisfaction or unhappiness with what is going on in our life. These feelings can arise from any number of sources but once they hit, life can become fairly uncomfortable.

For many, when they are impacted with this type of feeling they fall deeply into it. They allow their disparaging feelings to over take them. This can lead to all kinds of negative moods and behavior. Mostly, what it does is to keep someone locked into this state of unhappy emotion, awaiting, hoping for someone or something to come and shake them out of their funk.

But, as long as you are hoping for someone or something else to change what you are feeling, you have relinquished control of your life and your emotions over to the abstract nothing.

You can hope and wish forever, but if you do not actually do something, you may be locked into this attitude for a very long period of time.

Try this next time you find yourself hating life… First of all, step back from that feeling. Let go of it, if only for a moment. Do not let it dominate your mind.

Once you have done this, look out across where you live, (if this is where the feeling is taking control over you). Find something you like. Maybe it is some possession you own; perhaps it is a piece of art, maybe it is a photograph of a fun time in your life. Find that object and focus on it. Feel the happiness that object brings to your mind. Allow thinking about that object to remove you from the sense of dread that you are experiencing.

The feeling of unhappiness, dissatisfaction, and frustration does not only overtake people at home. Perhaps it may come on at your workplace. This is why wherever you find yourself on a daily basis you really need to bring things into that space that make you happy.

Sometimes, some people work in place where they do not have a desk or an office. For them, having some stationary item that brings them joy may be more difficult. For people in this position it is a good idea to find something that you like to wear that makes you feel a certain kind of way. Maybe it is a ring, a bracelet, a necklace, or a belt buckle. It can really be anything as long as when you need a new place to refocus your energy it can be there for you.

Some people live in beautiful homes. I know when I see them I think, *"Why can't I live in a place like that?"* Not everybody can afford to live in those seemingly perfect environments, however. But, we all live somewhere. What you need to do, wherever you live, is to make that space as much YOU as possible. Fill where you live, fill where you work, fill what you drive, with things that make you happy.

The more things that bring you happiness that you have around you, the more able you will be to focus on joy rather that focusing on that feeling that is taking you away from your moment and casting you into a state of unhappiness.

Never let a negative emotion take hold of your life. For the longer you feel it, the more control it has over you. When you experience dissatisfaction or unhappiness, as we all do from time to time, immediately catch yourself, let go of it, find that something that makes you happy, and focus on the happiness it brings you. Remember, as simply of an object as that item may be, it possesses all the power it the world if you allow it to take you back to a space of contentment.

* * *
25/Aug/2020 08:52 AM

What do you do when you have nothing to do?

The Things That People Say and What Do Your Words Actually Mean?
24/Aug/2020 05:25 PM

I always find in both interesting and curious when I hear someone speaking about some subject and what they are saying is completely wrong. It is not based in truth.

I forever find it interesting and strange that people say all kinds of things about people and subjects that they possess no true knowledge about but (to keep the conversation going) that misstate all kinds of false facts.

There is certainly nothing new about this. It has happened forever and ever. But, do you ever questions what you are saying and why? Do you ever question the basis of what you are proclaiming? Do you even care if what you are saying is factual? Or, is it good enough for you simply speak so you can be in the conversation? And, does it matter to you if what you are saying is false?

Do you ever actually listen to the things other people say? Do you ever truly read what someone else writes? Do you ever wonder if what they are saying is right and true or do you just immediately accept it as fact?

When many people listen to conversations, I believe that most do not truly care if what that other person is saying is true or not. But, don't you think that this is a flaw of humanity? Don't you think that someone should base what he or she says upon fact?

Certainly, there is the concept of interpretation and opinion. As we all understand, that's just one person stating what he or she thinks about that someone or that something else. For me, the problem arises when people state their opinions as a fact without defining it as such. In fact, very few proclaim their opinion to be just an opinion at the outset of a conversation. Again, here we find information being put out into the world as fact when it is not.

People do all kinds of things to turn what they believe into palatable information—information that may be accepted by others. But, if what they are saying is not fact, if it is not factually based, what does that information actually add to the ever-growing knowledge of humanity? What does it actually give to the world?

In some cases, facts are debatable. In some cases, facts are evolving. Under those circumstances, perhaps discussion is warranted, as decisions can be made upon new input and insight. But, most of the time it seems people just want to voice whatever comes to their mind; forget about if it is true or not.

I suppose I live in a bit of an interesting circumstance that provides me with a somewhat unique perspective into this situation, as sometimes people speak and/or write about me. I am really not one of those people who ever seeks this kind of stuff out as mostly I just don't want to know. But, every now and then I am confronted with it.

Due to my writings and my movies and stuff people seem to occasionally want to discuss my creations, my motivations, and myself. Sometimes those discussions are positive; sometimes they are not. Sometimes they are funny; sometimes they are mean spirited. But, the one thing I notice when I read or hear about what someone has said is, more often than not, they are simply wrong. They are stating facts about my creations, my inspirations, or my life that are just not true.

So, what does this tells us? What can we learn from this? I think the biggest thing is we really have to look deeply into our sense of self and decide what it is we want to do and why we desire to do it. Do we simply want to speak to speak, no matter whether what we are saying is true or not? Do we simply want our opinions to be heard as truths? Or, do we want to take the time to actually research a subject before we say anything and thereby make what we say as factual as possible?

Life is full of all kinds of beliefs. But, what are those beliefs based upon? What are your beliefs based upon? Do you believe what you hear simply because you have heard it? Or, do you seek the source of the knowledge, find out the actual facts, and then know what you know based upon the truth or at least as close as you can get to it as possible?

Think when you hear. Think when you read. Think before you believe.

You can say whatever it is you want to say. You can believe whatever it is you want to believe. But, if what you are saying is not the truth, what are you saying, what are you believing, and what do your words actually mean?

* * *
24/Aug/2020 10:00 AM

What happens when what you think is wrong?

What happens when what you say is wrong?

What happens when what you do is wrong?

* * *

24/Aug/2020 09:22 AM

Who would you rather be, the person who says something positive or says something negative?

Who would you rather be, the person who does something positive or does something negative?

Who would you rather be, the person who helps someone or hurts someone?

In every moment of your life you can make a choice about what you are going to do next.

Everybody Lies
23/Aug/2020 03:17 PM

Here's a brief segment from my book *Zen Filmmaking* that I hope may be helpful to some of you filmmakers out there.

The number one rule of filmmaking is…

"Everybody Lies."

I generally lead into this point in a much more poetic manner than simply stating it so boldly as I have done here—sighting references, etc. But, to begin any understanding of filmmaking, you must initially understand this point.

What Does It Mean?

The question can be asked, *"What does this mean—Everybody Lies?"*

The answer is very simple, in filmmaking, people lie about every aspect of their life, their experience, their production, what they have, have-not, will-not, or can-not do. Mostly, people lie to make their production and/or their resume look bigger and better than it is.

What they lie about and why they do it is as unique as the individual. But, there are some commonalities in what lies are perpetrated across the industry. To go down the list:

Actors tend to lie about the fact that they have been in films. They may make up titles that do not exist in order to make their resume look stronger. Or, they may amplify the size of the role they had in any indie or student film to increase their desirability. In addition, actors commonly claim that they were a part of large A-Film. The fact commonly is, however, that these people were at best extras in these films.

Film crewmembers lie about their experience; what they can do and how they can help the production with their knowledge. One of the most notorious things that partially cameramen do is to say that they know how to load and to use a particular camera when they do not but this fact is not revealed until they are on the set. It is also quite common for a cameraman to agree to work with limited lighting and then either the night before or the day of the shoot proclaim that they cannot work with the lighting provided and you must either rent lighting from them or one of their friend if you want them to shoot the movie.

In terms of the lies that filmmakers tell—they are notorious for making all kinds of claims about their productions. They commonly falsify their production budget. They lie about the notoriety of what actor or actress was in their film. They lie about what format the film was shot on, where they shot their film, etc...

Film Distributors make all kinds of promises about what they will do with your film if you sign over the distribution rights to them. They may claim they will have it shown in theatres, distribute it in large video rental chains, or get it to the executives at the large studios. I cannot be firmer in explaining this; film distributors have one motivating factor in mind—making money for themselves. To accomplish this, they will lie to the filmmaker at all imaginable levels. They will not tell them what countries purchased rights to the film, they will create costs that never existed and claim that is why the filmmaker is due no monetary compensation, they will short-change or completely disavow any payment due to the filmmaker, and this is just the short-list. The number of filmmakers I have personally known who have created a feature film that received distribution and received no money or actually ended up owing the distribution company money is so large that it is almost ridiculous. But, that is a fact of the industry. And, it is a fact that you need to know.

At the end of the day people involved in the filmmaking process lie. The reason I explain this is that you, the filmmaker, needs to understand this and take this factor into consideration at the outset of entering into the filmmaking game. You need to do this in order to keep yourself from falling prey to a lie that may affect the overall outcome of your film and your overall psychological well-being.

Accusations Are a Dangerous Game
23/Aug/2020 11:17 AM

  Over the past couple of years there has been an abundance of accusations flying around. In fact, particularly in the entertainment industry and its various offshoots, a lot of people have been claiming a lot of things. Certainly, from the #metoo movement forward, a lot of people have leveled a lot of claims at a lot of people. The problem is, accusations are only that. They are not proven facts. They are simply somebody saying something about a person and from that a lot of damage can be created for that accused person; whether what is being said is true or not.

  When you hear an allegation about a person do you immediately believe it? If you do, that means that you are not an analytical person who actually seeks the truth. You are simply a believer. Though it is certainly much easier to be just a believer but for the person who follows that path there is never a sense of true realization. Thus, what is said by someone else, for who knows what reason, becomes the only knowledge had. From this, falsehoods have the potential to become accepted truths, even if they are not.

  I have occasionally written about the #metoo movement and other accusation-based factions since it appeared. As explained a few years ago in a blog, I too can claim #metoo at the hands of a female manager and a couple of female casting agents. But, more than just that, there is always another level that must be studied when listening to the accusation-filled words of someone. What is their motivation for saying what they were saying?

And, what part did they play in the overall outcome of what took place?

As we have seen, some of the people leveling accusations, in this period of history, have come to be found out as a person who they, themselves, did some very unsavory activities. The fact of the matter is, who hasn't? Who has not done something to someone that the person did not like, appreciate, or desire? That alone should make a person question who they truly are before they go out and level indictments against others.

Also, one must always question what does the person leveling accusations gain from the process? If you look to some of the most boisterous voices of recent years, what they have done is to cause their name to be brought back into the limelight as it had faded. Others have made large sums of money via writing articles or a book. In other cases, these actions have proven to be a means for a person to attack someone in the public eye for the accuser not receiving what they had hoped to gain from that individual. Whatever the case, a person's motivations must forever be questioned whenever they step up to the pulpit and accuse anyone of anything. This is particularly the case if they are condemning more than one individual.

Finally, does the person who is making accusations ever question their own responsibility it what took place? Here lies one of the most compelling questions that must be pondered. If a person says, *"No,"* and they are forced to do something that they do not want to do, the fault is very clear. But, how many people say, *"Yes,"* but regret their decision the next day, the next year, or later in their life? Whose fault is it if a person says, *"Yes?"* Whose fault is it if a person willingly takes part it an activity, whatever that activity may be? All of these questions and more must be pondered before any allegation should ever be believed.

I know in the world of the modern martial arts, accusations fly around all the time. People are attacked as to their training, their rank, their authority to teach, their skillset, and all of that kind of stuff. But, what are any of those accusations based upon? Answer: Only an attempt to discredit someone with some self-motivated logic. Again, you must really question who is saying what and why.

This goes to the point and the question in all accusations; can you be clear enough in your own open-mindedness to not judge before you actually and personally know all of the fact? Or, do you simply want to believe everything you hear?

If you are one of those people who immediately wants to believe the worst about anyone/everyone, what does that say about your character? If you are making accusations about someone to raise your name in public interest or to make money, what does that say about you as a human being? If you are a person who makes accusations about someone and you willingly took part in whatever activity your are casting your dispersions upon, what does that say about you as a person?

There's the great Tim McGraw song that has the lyric, *"You aint gotta dig too deep if you wanta find some dirt on me."* That's a great way to be honest about your life. For me, I've always attempted to follow that mindset via my novels, short stories, poetry, prose, and even in this blog. Be honest with who you truly are, what you have or have not done, and then you're the one telling your own life truths.

Nobody is perfect. We have all made mistakes. We have all hurt other people. It is what you do to never do that again that makes you the person you are to ultimately become. It is what you do to fix the damage you created that sets the ultimate definition for your life.

As for those who cast accusations, always ask yourself, *"Why are they saying what they are saying?"* Always question, *"What part did they play in the creating of the situation and the outcome?"* If they were a willing participant, then who is truly to blame?

If Only You Didn't Know
21/Aug/2020 10:09 AM

Think about something that really upset you. Think about something that you were really angry about. Why did that thing upset you?

There is one constant variable in this question. That is, you know about the situation and because you knew about it, you became distraught. But, what if you didn't know about it? It would not have made you angry.

In life, people get angry about all kinds of things. Certainly, there are the very obvious causations of irritation. Somebody says or does something to you face-to-face that you really do not like. Those anger-creating moments are very physical. They are generally person-to-person. That's where fights break out and all that kind of stuff. But, most of the other things that upset a person are very abstract. Somebody heard something about someone else saying or doing something and from that anger is generated in their being.

Think about the times you have been sent to anger when it was not caused by a face-to-face experience. In those moments, what were you angry about? Most likely, someone told you something about what someone else said or did; maybe you read about it or maybe you even heard about it on the news. Whatever the causation factor, had you not found out about it, what would you have been feeling? Non-anger, obviously.

But, you did hear about it—you did find out about it. Now what?

One of the facts of life is, people choose what they become angry about. What makes one person angry does not affect another person in that same way. So, I can say, just don't let anger overtake you. But, few people have the capacity to not become pissed off when someone does something that they do not like.

Many people, however, become very upset over situations that have nothing to do with them on a personal level. These are the people who are seeking out anger. They are looking for something to become angry about. There is something missing in their life and they are constantly looking outside of themselves for something to motivate their emotions. This is a very low level of human consciousness but it is very common.

The main thing to keep in mind is what you have to do when you begin to feel anger arising in you is you must question how does what that other person said or did actually affect you and your life? Yes, you may not like what they said or did, but does their words or their actions directly affect your life in any significant manner? If so, then you have a basis for anger. If not, let it go.

The fact of life is, (and you see and hear about it all the time), people are very self-motivated in their words and actions and they do things in order to take control over the emotions, the minds, and the actions of other people. It is a control thing. Thus, people say and do things that will cause people to react. And, many times they do these things based upon a very selfish, uncaring mindset. Yet, they do them nonetheless.

I believe we have all encountered people that have said things about us or done things to us that made us angry. In many cases, what they said were lies or misrepresentations of our intentions. In other cases, what they did was really selfishly motivated. But, they did it nonetheless. And, we are the one left to process the repercussions.

The truly mentally refined individual can just dismiss these negative words and actions and cast them to the knowledge of their own inner knowledge; knowing what is right and true. In other cases, people do things that must be responded to because what they have done has truly personally hurt someone's life. But, the fact of any response, based in anger or otherwise, means it only escalates the situation. It causes more people to know about it and more people to become involved with it, leading to who knows what?

As I say over and over again, people are a very selfish breed. They think predominately about themselves; their own level of life and world reality and they rarely take anyone else into consideration. Even people who become angry over what was done to someone else generally only care because they care about the person that something was done to. Thus, their emotions are a selfish reaction.

All life is based upon action—what one person does to another person. If you didn't know about what anyone else was saying or doing, you would have no reason to become angry. This is why people have retreated from the world for eons. But, for most of us, we must interact with the world. We must deal with the stupid shit some people say and do. The best way to free yourself from the controlling hands of anger is to not care if you find out about what someone may have said or done. …Know that they are only in for themselves—they are only thinking about themselves. Jealousy, envy, judgmentalness, and unrequited love retribution, all of these are motivating motivators for negative words and deeds, as are a lot more.

Anger only can overtake you if you allow it to overtake you. If you don't know, you don't know. If you can cast it from your mind because you realize the limited perceptions of the person seeking a response, do so. If you can't, never let the words or the actions of others define who and what you are to become. Be more than a person who is less than you. Allow the anger in you to be released, never let it take control.

If you don't know, you don't know. There lies life perfection. If you do not know, then you know. But, it is you who chooses what to do with that information. Always embrace the Higher Self. Always be the best you can be. Be strong enough to let it go and forget. Embrace goodness, happiness, truth, and rightness. Let go and know.

Locked Into a Pattern of Life Equals Time Killing or Killing Time?
20/Aug/2020 07:35 AM

You are born. You live. You die. What is in between is all that you have. What is in your in between? What have you done? What are you doing? Why are you doing it? And, do you ever contemplate any of this?

There is no choice in life but to pass from birth to death. Most people attempt to fill that time with feeling as All Right as they are allowed. But, the fact of life is, we are all destine to live with the options that we are provided with. We are all defined by our circumstance. This being said, there is personal choice. There are the choices we each make with the choices we are given.

What choices have you made that have come to define your life? And, how have the choices you have made come to define your life, the life of those you have encountered, and the greater world as a whole?

Very few people contemplate their life choices. They simply make them as they are presented. They never analyze the deeper implications of what they do and why they do it. They simply make a choice between the obvious choices that they are provided with.

How about you? Do you ever study your choices? Do you ever analyze why those choices were provided to you? Do you ever study how those choices have shaped your life and how they have come to shape the life of others you have encountered?

Most people must find a means of survival. This unusually means finding a way to make a living; i.e. a job. For many, their job becomes the entire primary focus of their life. Though they may have their hopes, their dreams, their family, and their vacations, all of those things are predicated upon the fact that they must earn a living. Thus, all other things in life are surround by the time they must put in and the things they must do at the work place. How about you? How does you job affect your life?

For many, if you watch their patterns of behavior, their job is like a drug. They can do all kinds of things outside of the job. They can help people. They can hurt people. They can help or hurt themselves, but their primary focus is that all important job. For no matter what they do in their life, they know that come the AM (or whenever) they must show up at the work place and it is there where their life will be provided with that all important, all encompassing, drug of monetary existence.

Certainly, as they world has evolved, particularly in the past few decades with the birth of the internet, the workplace may look very different than it did in times gone past. Some people make their living on the internet. Though this may be the case, does the addictive drug of their job change? No. As they must make a living, it does not. They may go out and do a million other things but the focusing drug of their job always brings them back to the central concentration of that job.

The job is where many of the problems of living a good and a productive life arise. Because, no matter what your job is, how much you love or you hate your job, it is an all-encompassing reality. It is your drug. It is the thing that you do day in and day out. As such, it becomes the same drug with the same effect. You do what you do what you do everyday until you can do it no more. Nothing ever changes.

Even with the few people who make their living via thing like being a personality or presenting a show on the internet, what they do never changes. That person is that thing and that is what the do. Thus, there is never any growth.

Look at any person in any job. Who were they when they began that job? Who are they now? It is safe to say, nothing has changed. Even look at any internet celebrity. Who were they when they began that job? Who are they now? Nothing has truly changed. They are the same person doing the same thing with no life evolution. And, this is where the damnation of the drug/of the addiction to the work place has ruined so many lives and the lives of so many people who are dominated by the job of that other person. There is no chance for evolution!

Now, there is an essential point to understand. The lack of evolution is a personal choice. And, the fact of the matter is, most people will argue that they have changed, that they have evolved through time. But, all you have to do is to look at who they were then, compared to who they are now; what they were doing then, compared to what they are doing now; how they were behaving then, compared to how they were behaving now, how they were treating others then, compared to how they are treating others now, and the answer to the truth about their evolution, or lack thereof, will become very clear.

Getting older is not evolving. It is just getting older. Changing the clothes you wear or altering your hairstyle is not evolving it is just a physical change defined by who and what is pushing the current trends. Personal evolution is truly growing on an interpersonal psychological and spiritual level. This is what most people never do.

So, what are you doing? Why are you doing it? How are you doing it? How is what you are doing, doing to others? And, do you ever even think about any of this?

You can be forced to make only the obvious choices you are present with in your life. You can be controlled by all that is outside of your control. You can make excuses for your all and your everything and why you do what you do and why you have done what you have done. But, if you do not become consciously involved in the elemental activities and the doings of your life, all you have done is to release control to the hands of your destiny and your unthinking mind and all you will be allowing is your life to have become defined by the practice of making only the choices your are allowed to make.

Do more with your life. Think. Don't allow the addiction of the workplace to dominate your existence. Become more. Do more. Spread a conscious positivity outwards from your inner being. Then, when death comes knocking at your door, as it does for all of us, your life will have actually meant something. You will not have simply released control of your life to the obviousness of the choices you were allowed to make based upon addictions you allowed yourself to develop.

* * *
19/Aug/2020 12:09 PM

How much of what you believe you know is based upon what you've experienced compared to what you have heard from others?

* * *
19/Aug/2020 06:59 AM

Should you care about a person who doesn't care about you?

* * *
18/Aug/2020 12:14 PM

Everybody's God is different. You may refer to him by the same name but your interpretation of God is uniquely your own.

* * *
18/Aug/2020 07:44 AM

As long as your mind is focused on something outside of yourself your mind is not focused on yourself and making yourself the best person that you can become.

* * *
17/Aug/2020 08:58 AM

If you clean it before it becomes dirty it will forever be clean.

What Have You Stolen?
16/Aug/2020 10:21 AM

What have you stolen in life? What have you taken from someone without their consent?

Most people when they steal something from someone never take the other person into consideration. They do not consider how that item being stolen will make that other person feel. They do not contemplate how if that item were stolen from them how it would make them feel.

Most people when they steal place all kinds of justifications upon their actions. Some claim poverty. Some claim empowerment. Some claim retribution. But, whatever the thief is claiming, that does not take away from the fact that they took something that was not theirs.

How many thieves refer to themselves as a thief? How many people who steal even contemplate how what they are doing will affect that someone else?

Here lays one the primary problems with humanity. Many people only think about themselves. They only think about what they want. They only think about devising a method to get what they want. Then, once they have it, they never even contemplate what their thievery did to the life of that other person.

Some people are good. They think and they care about that other person. They contemplate how their actions may affect them. Many others are not like that, however. They steal, they take, they do it simply because they can get away with it and they only process what they have done if they are caught and taken to task for their action and then, at best, all they do is to mount a defense as to why they did what they did. In fact, some even become angry with the person that they stole from when they are confronted by the individual.

Again, what have you stolen? Who have you stolen from? How did that stealing action affect your life? How did that stealing action affect the life of the person you took that something from?

Take a moment right now. Take out a piece of paper and make a list of the items you have stolen—things that you took that were not knowingly and willingly given to you. What did those items mean to your life then? What do they mean to your life now? How did that stealing affect your life? How did that stealing affect the life of the person whom you stole that item from?

If you don't think about the other person, you are a selfish individual. Some take pride in that fact. But, as we all can agree, that is not an honorable thing to form a basis for pride.

If you make excuses for what you have done and what you are doing, those excuses do not change the fact of what you have done. They simply allow you to find an internal remedy for the truth about what your actions are actually creating.

This is your life; how you live it will define your reality. How you live it will define how other people will judge you. How you live it will define what comes next and next and next in your life.

You can steal if you want. But, if you steal, don't you agree, that someone will be hurt by that action? Is that what you want, to hurt other people?

Stop making excuses for your action and everything in everybody's life becomes just a little bit better. Think about how your actions will affect that other person and everything in their life becomes a little bit better.

Who do you want to be? What do you want to be known as? A thief or a person who cares enough to put their own desires on hold and never takes anything from anybody that is not freely given? Your life. Your choice.

* * *
16/Aug/2020 08:34 AM

If one word provides enough of an explanation why use a hundred?

*　　*　　*
16/Aug/2020 08:00 AM

If all you think about is how you are feeling then you are missing the entire point of human understanding.

*   *   *

16/Aug/2020 07:58 AM

If what you did to someone one minute ago, one day ago, one year ago, or one lifetime ago is still affecting them why do you think you will still not be receiving the karmic repercussions?

* * *
16/Aug/2020 07:57 AM

If you tell someone what to do and they do it all outcomes are your responsibility.

* * *
16/Aug/2020 07:56 AM

If you remove what you want out of every life situation that situation is allowed to evolve into its own perfection.

* * *
16/Aug/2020 07:56 AM

If you don't know how to do something it's better that you don't do it.

* * *
14/Aug/2020 09:46 AM

Just because you don't believe it doesn't mean it isn't true.

It's Called Fixing It
13/Aug/2020 09:44 AM

Picking up from a blog I wrote the other day, we all make mistakes. We all do things that we didn't necessarily mean to do, just as we all sometimes do those unconscious somethings that hurts the life of someone else. What defines us, as a human being, is what we do after that action. …What we do after the fact that attempts to repair the mistake(s) we made.

Some people are locked into a mindset of selfishness. The process of thinking, *"I am right and you are wrong."* Thus, they don't care about any damage they unleash. Other people are locked into the mindset of denial. They don't really think or care about anyone else but themselves so they could care less of what they did that hurt the life of someone else. Still others, even though they may have accidentally hurt someone never want to own what they have done, they never want to be the one who is blamed, they never want to be the one who must say, *"I'm sorry,"* so they exist in a state of denial, leading to lies, so they will not have to take responsibility for their action whether consciously undertaken or not. In each of these cases we are left with one person doing one thing, that hurt the life of someone else, and that person is not doing anything to make it better.

I believe that we all have been on the wrong side of someone else actions and what that person has done to us has left our life, our emotions, or our life evolution hurt in either a small or a large manner. In these cases, it is only natural, for us on the receiving end, to hope that the doing person will say or do something to make us feel better. And, in some cases they do. That is the right thing to do. But, in other cases, the enacting person is so locked into a mindset of selfishness that they either do nothing or find some misplaced logic to justify their action.

People either live their life from a position of caring and giving or they live their life from a position of wanting and taking. There really is no in-between. Because what a person does, how they do it, and how they react to the results illustrates their mental makeup. They take or they give. They care or they do not. They feel remorse or they deny.

The reason there is so much chaos in the word, so much hurt, so many hurt feelings, so many lives interrupted, is that many people operate from a perspective of selfishness. Even when they do something wrong, whether it is an accidental action or not, they do not acknowledge their responsibility it what has occurred. And, this goes to all levels of life from hurt feelings onto murder. If a person believes they are right in what they have done, if a person feels no remorse for what they have done, if a person takes pride in what they have done, there is nothing that you can say or do that will make them change their mind. So, where does this leave us?

Yes, we all hope that when someone hurts us, they will acknowledge their actions, say they are sorry, and try to fix what they have broken. But, this is a hope so commonly dashed by the inaction of so many doers.

In some cases, a person's lack of moral sympathy causes the hurt individual to react to the initial action. Thus, they do something to hurt that person who hurt them. Then, the initial hurtful action becomes amplified, actions-upon-action, and who knows where it will end? Usually nowhere good.

Hurt only equals hurt. It's really as simple as that. Negative reaction to negative action only amplifies the negativity. I can say, *"Don't do things that will hurt someone else."* I can suggest, *"If you accidentally do something that has hurt someone be sorry for your actions and try to repair the damage."* But, if you are one of those people who does not care about the person you hurt, I doubt that those words will make you care. And, that is sad, because you did hurt someone and you should fix what you have done.

Life is an interplay of people and personalities. It is an interchange of action and reaction. Each person is who each person is. Each person feels what each person feels. Each person cares about what each person cares about. You care about what you care about and that should provide you with the insight to understand that everybody feels, everybody can be hurt, and that hurt never feels good; it is never a good thing.

Be more than your temporary action: accidental or otherwise. Feel for the other person. Understand they too have feelings. If you hurt them, fix it. If they hurt you, and they won't try to fix it, forgiven them, forget about them, because there is nothing that you can do to make them the higher level individual that you hoped that they could be.

Sādhanā
13/Aug/2020 07:47 AM

Sādhanā is the Sanskrit word that refers to refined spiritual discipline. It references the formalized practices that one must undertake to reach a higher state of consciousness.

How much time to you spend consciously refining your anything? How much time to you intentionally spend attempting to make yourself a better, more cultivated individual? The answer for most is that they spend no time at all. They do nothing that is focused on them becoming a more developed human being. Yes, they may go to school so they can get a good job. Yes, they may investigate and may learn how to do that something so that they can make more money. But, very few ever do anything that will lead to making themselves a truly illuminated being?

Why is that? Most probably because it is an abstract idea. Higher consciousness does not commonly lead to making more money, gaining more fame, getting more followers on social media. In fact, it leads to nothing. …That spiritual nothing that is so illusive. Because of this fact, very few possess the mind to perform Sādhanā.

For example, in the martial arts, I have known numerous people who really fall in love with the physical training. They train day in and day out. But, in the martial arts there is a goal; a higher belt rank that may lead to personal gratification, a sense of self-worth, more students, and thus more money and notoriety. That is a physical thing that a person is given the motivation to work towards. But, working hard towards making one's self a better vehicle of enlightenment promises very little—very little at least in terms of the physical world.

Some people do make enlightenment the goal. From this, there are a very few who do work hard at Sādhanā. They meditate for long periods of time. They chant for hours. But, enlightenment is not a goal. That is why so few people ever truly understand it. And, that is why it is the most illusive element of human consciousness. It is not a thing. It is not a place. It is not something that can be worked for and then earned. It simply is.

If this is the case, some may ask, why perform Sādhanā at all? Why? Because consciously becoming that something more refined not only makes the individual a better person but it makes them a more positive conduit for the betterment of everything. It makes them a vehicle to make everything and everyone just a little bit better.

Ask yourself, *"What do you think about?"* Ask yourself, *"What do you do to make yourself a better person?"* Ask yourself, *"Do you care enough about the everyone out there to formally do something that will cause you to increase your consciousness, thereby limiting your selfishness, your unthinkingness, and your negative actions, thereby leaving everything and everyone just a little bit better?"*

Sādhanā is not just about someone doing something. It is not a selfish, self-thinking act. Sādhanā is a person caring enough to work towards making themselves that something better so that everything can exist in a space of betterment.

How about you? What spiritual practices are you willing to undertake to make everything just a little bit better?

The Mistakes You Make Affects the Life of Other People
12/Aug/2020 09:19 AM

We all male mistakes. That's just the reality of life. We all say and do things that we should not have done. But, we did them anyway.

When we make a mistake, it is the general attitude that we think about ourselves. We think how we messed up what we hoped to do or what we hoped to achieve. But, how often do you think about how your mistakes affected the life of that someone else?

The fact of life is, we are not alone in this universe. There are other people. Do you ever consider the fact that when you make a mistake you are not only affecting you but you are affecting the life of someone else? And, more importantly, do you care?

Think about a mistake you made. Maybe it was something you said; maybe it was something you did. …Really, mistakes come in many shapes and sizes. Now, think about how you felt when you made that mistake. What did you think about it? How did it make you feel? How did it affect your life? And, in all of that thinking, did you think about anyone else? Did you contemplate how what you said or what you did affected the life of someone else? Or, did you dismiss their feeling—how what you did affected them, as you were lost in only the contemplation of you?

No person is an island. No person is completely alone. Even if you made a mistake that seemingly only messed up your life, there were still other people involved. Did the thought of them ever cross your mind?

In life, some people intentionally set out to hurt or damage the life of other people. They do this via words and actions. Those are not mistakes. Those are conscious activities. But sometimes, some people are conscious enough to realize that what they said about a person was wrong, what they did to a person what not right. It was a mistake. Then what? When you have encountered this type of a life situation what have you done to repair your mistake? Have you done anything?

Most/many life mistakes just happen. We did not anticipate their occurrence so we could not prepare for their prevention. But, when they do happen, where is your consciousness? Is it only on you or is it also on anyone/everyone else involved?

We all mistakes. We all (sometimes) do stupid stuff. But, it is what you do on the tail end of that mistake that defines the type of person you truly are.

Do you lie to cover up your mistakes? Do you try to place the blame on someone else? Or, do you own your mistake and try to repair any damage you have created, not only for your own life but also for the life of anyone else involved?

Mistake can come to be the defining factor of a person's life. How do you react when you make a mistake?

Why Did You Dream What You Dreamt Last Night?
11/Aug/2020 07:41 AM

Why did you dream what you dreamt last night? Why did you live that experience in your mind's eye?

Seemingly forever, people have contemplated their dreams. There have been books written attempting to define what a specific dream means. Psychotherapists attempt to analyze a person via their dreams. But, all of these activities are only a guess at best. They are generally wrong.

Many people, through out time, have written their autobiography. They detail the detailings of their life. Even if they don't write it down, everybody pretty much remembers various events in their life. Think about it, if you were to write an autobiography of your dreams, what a grand life you would have live.

Think about your dreams. Think about the things you have lived in your dreams—the great and the grand experiences that you lived there but you have never lived in so call, *"Real life."* But, you did live those experiences. You did live them in your dreams. While you were dreaming were those experiences any less real? Why can't you write an autobiography of the life you lived in your dreams?

Most people don't take note of their dreams. They don't really remember most of them. But, they are going on all the time when you sleep.

Most people only remember their dreams for the few minutes when their vividness is active when they first wake up. Sometimes they were very intense and then they may even be discussed with a family member or a friend. But, in virtually all cases, they are then forgotten.

You dream almost as much as you live, *"Real life."* Shouldn't your dreams be more than simply a forgotten nothing?

True to the Tradition
10/Aug/2020 08:26 AM

There is traditional and then there is non-traditional. There is formalized and then there is eclectic. There is established and then there is radicalized.

In life… In the rituals of life, there are those who follow a formalized pattern of dissemination and then there are those who take a little bit of this, a little bit of that, and congregate all of these elements into one interconnected whole. Though that whole may be considered a formalized something, it is not based in any long standing tradition and, thus, its foundational wisdom must be questioned.

I was watching the multi-part documentary about Charles Manson last night on the Epix network. Though, at least for me, as I long ago studied the life and doings of Charles Manson, there was not a lot of new information but the networks presentation of the events are done so in an interesting manner.

In last night segment, they were discussing Manson's emersion into the San Francisco, *"Hippie,"* culture of 1967. The documentary discussed how there were many, *"Gurus,"* teaching and seeking a flock at that point in history in San Francisco. Though I was young at that point in time, I remember that time period very well. These disciple-seeking teachers were proclaiming very much the same things, *"Your family doesn't understand you, I do." "Drop out and turn on," "I'm not me, I'm just your mirror," "Let go and know," "There is no sin,"* and the all of that kind of mumbo-jumbo. For the seeker—for the person dissatisfied with society and their life, it all sounded pretty good. It promised a grand illusion. It all made a promise of that illusive, *"Something else."* But, where did all of those people (if they are still alive) end up? They ended up living the nine-to-five of the reality of reality even if they may have held on to some of their idealistic illusions.

Here lies the problem when people attempt to create a new philosophy-based reality based upon a mishmash of established traditions. All it is, is that; a mishmash of someone's interpretation of someone else's something. It is not an established based tradition. It is not rooted in centuries of cultural exploration. It is just somebody who heard or read something that they liked the sound of, spitting it out, and proclaiming it as their own. But, it is not their own. It is not based in tradition. It is just a bunch of stuff thrown into the blender, mixed up, and served to whomever would drink the concoction.

From my perspective, as a person who followed that path of higher realization, made popular in that era of American history, I always studied from Eastern born teachers. I studied from teachers, who themselves, had studied at the source. Thus, I felt I might gain the true essence of the tradition. This is the same with my studies of the martial arts. I always studied from Asian born and trained teachers. I studied from teachers who were taught at the sourcepoint. Again, believing that this was the best way to gain a complete and traditional understanding.

Were all of these teachers perfect? No, of course not. Just like everyone, some of them had some serious flaws. But, what they did offer was a pathway to gain knowledge from the sourcepoint—from the essence of where the tradition originated.

In life, there always has been and there always will be those people who hope to be seen as a teacher. There has always been those people who seek students and disciples to stroke their ego. But, if a person cannot demonstrate a pathway of their knowledge being gained from its source, if they cannot illustrate how they are linked to the traditional home of an established anything, if all they are doing is taking a little of this and mixing it up with a little bit of that and claiming that they are the true sourcepoint of a unique form of higher knowledge then all they actually are is a misguided individual with no basis in true knowledge seeking nothing more than to be something they are not.

Think about whom you are studying under before you ever listen to a word they say. Do this to not only protect yourself but to protect others from what these self-proclaimed people may do to damage your life and the life and the world of others.

*   *   *

10/Aug/2020 08:26 AM

Do you take time out of your day everyday to take care of someone else?

A Question of Morality
09/Aug/2020 07:34 AM

Lets face facts; a lot of people do a lot of bad things. People do a lot of hurtful things that damage the life of other people. They most commonly do these things with an unthinking, uncaring mind and if they are not doing them to intentionally hurt a specific individual they are doing them to gain some undescribed sense of something that can only be felt by themselves. But, no matter what may be the case of causation and desired outcome, one thing that can be sure is that what they are doing is done from a sense of a lack of wholeness and a lack of conscious empathy.

People who do bad things in their late adolescence and adulthood almost universally have done bad things in their younger years. It is very uncommon to find a person who has done one very bad something who has never done anything like that before. Whether that negative deed they perform is based thievery, violence, or promiscuity, what they do they have done before.

This is the thing that one must really study when they come to be in any kind of a relationship with an individual. They must truly look to the past of that person and explore the things that they have previously done because it is almost universally guaranteed that what they have done in the past they will do again. Though it may not be exactly the same action, it will be of a similar nature where that person will go against the laws of what is right and what is good.

Certainly, it has long been established that an individual behaves in a manner that was illustrated and taught to them in their youth. If a child grew up in an abusive household, it is very common for them to be physically or verbally abusive in their later relationships. If a child witnessed stealing, they will commonly follow in the footsteps of their parents. If a child grew up with parents or in a family who excessively used intoxicants, they too can be expected to walk down that road. If a child was exposed to judgmental, critical words and behavior, they too will act in that fashion. If a child saw promiscuity they too will act out in this manner, and so on.

When an individual who follows a different path from this and was exposed to different, more positive, formative years encounters a person who behaves in a less than ideal manner, they may believe and/or suggest that the individual obtain counseling or psychotherapy. The fact is, though this type of cognitive treatment is much more available in this time and place in history, it is also not readily available to most. First of all, in many cases, depending on a person's cultural circumstances, it is difficult to seek out. Moreover, it generally costs money. Money that a good percentage of the population does not posses. So, to simply suggest something like that, and assume that a person can easily follow through, is not as easy as it sounds.

The fact is, from the outside looking in, it is easy to comment on all kinds of things about another individual but until you have taken a moment to walk in their shoes, and live what they have lived, you can never truly understand anything about them. And, this is one of the root points of human consciousness and the defining of other people; if you are not them, you can never truly understand them. You can cast your judgment, but judgment is only that, it is not the truth. It is not what a person understands to be reality in their own mind.

Here, we come back to the fact that certain people do a certain type of thing. Though the actual causation factors may be many, and never truly fully understood by anyone, if a person has followed a path of less than acceptable behavior, it is almost guaranteed that is integrated as a formational element of that individual and they will do bad things again.

What can be learned from this? Perhaps the most basic understanding is that a person is who they are. At their elemental core, they are that certain something. Yes, some people can truly evolve away from that something that they used to be, but those people are very few and very far between. Most people either never see the need for change, they are not mentally aware enough to understand a need of change, or they are too unaware about the needs of another person or persons to care enough to change. Maybe they take pride and gain sustenance in their bad behavior. Or, maybe their bad behavior makes them feel good in some way known only to them.

Life is an individual process. What you feel is only felt by you. What you do may affect someone else or a large group as a whole, but the fact of life is, one person decides to do one thing. If that one thing leaves all things better, that is a good thing. If that one thing hurts anyone, including one's self, that is a bad thing. But, how few are the people who contemplate any of this. Most just do what they do, guided only by their momentary emotions and they do not care who it impacts as long as they feel okay.

Remember, people are who they are throughout their lifetime. What they did then, they will do again. Make sure you are willing to have them do that, once upon a time something, because it is almost a universal truth that who a person was yesterday, deep down inside, they are still that person today.

*   *   *
08/Aug/2020 02:07 PM

Jesus doesn't call you a sinner it is only someone who claims to speak on behalf of Jesus who does.

* * *

08/Aug/2020 07:40 AM

In a dream, no matter how realistic, if a negative life event occurs you can wake up and forget about it. In life, if a negative event finds you, it is you who must actually deal with it. How you deal with negative life events can come to be the definition of your life.

* * *
07/Aug/2020 01:41 PM

No religious or political mandate can tell you what's right or wrong but if you take a vow and you break it you are the one in the wrong.

Lighting the Front Man
07/Aug/2020 10:23 AM

I was watching TV in the late night the other night and I found myself viewing some music videos on, *"I want my 80s"* on MTV Classic. The video for, *"Carless Whispers,"* by Wham came on. Though I've seen that video a million times from the 1980s forward, I became quite transfixed on this one image where you view the back of George Michaels and he has this great rim light around him. The perfection of that lighting got me to thinking about a whole lot of things…

First of all, it was done in an era when music videos cost a lot of money to produce, and I guess this one had its share of problems. But, more than that, the only member of Wham you see in the video is George Michaels. Where's Andrew Ridgeley? Why is he not in it? I don't know? But, like other ego driven front men like say Andre 3000 of Outkast or Adam Levine of Maroon 5 you will see music videos of the band where they are the only featured member. I guess the people who actually create the music don't matter. But, I suppose that is a whole other issue and topic…

BTW Back in '85 (I think) I accidentally ended up staying in the same hotel in Guangzhou when Wham were passing through on what was apparently a ground breaking tour of China. Again, I guess that's another story.

But lighting… Especially when it is really good truly takes the viewer of anything to a different level. It is really an art form onto itself. Especially when it is so dramatic like that rim shot in that music video. Shots like that really take a lot of work to create.

In my films, I have, especially in the interior shots, tried to create visually interesting lighting situations. But, really good cost a lot of money. So, I've mostly had to live with what I could get.

I think back to this one time, and I discuss this in my book, *Independent Filmmaking, Secrets of the Craft,* when my DP was just fighting me tooth and nail about the lighting. I've always liked highly colored gel shots for my interior scenes. I get 'em when I can. But, I wanted to go red for this one bedroom scene in one of my Zen Films and I don't know if the guy didn't have the skillset or what, but to even get him to put a red gel on the Fresnel was like pulling teeth. Anyway…

Another case I think to was when Don Jackson and I were doing *Roller Blade Seven.* We were shooting at the garage studio of one of our cameramen. You may not know this but a lot of indie film people have shooting stages permanently set up in their garage. Anyway, this was for the scene where Don's character and mine have our talk that sends Hawk on his mission, *"You mean my sister that became your sister?"* We had talked to the camera guy and our art director about how we wanted separate, very distinctive, beams of light to stream in. We bought some foam core board to orchestrate this and they told us they could do it. We went and grabbed a burger and came back. But, when we sat down in the scene, there was just ambient light coming through the too many holes they had cut. It was not what we had envisioned at all.

Here lies the problem with lack of funds and less then competent people in the world of low budget filmmaking or anything in life for that matter. You can only get what you can get out of a person. They can't give you what they can't give you even enough most will claim that they can. And, unless you have the money to pay to have something done properly, the way you envision it, you will most likely have to live with what you can get out of them.

You know, there is really a lot of perfect perfection out there. But one, you have to have the developed senses to see it and understand it. And two, you have to either develop the ability yourself to create it or possess enough money to pay to have it actualized if you are living in the world of creativity.

All of life is pretty average. It is what you see everyday and it is what you have seen a millions times before. But, every now and then there is that moment of enlightening perfection. Maybe you see it. Maybe you want to create it. But, if you don't have the people surrounding you that can help you get to that plateau, more than likely all you will be left with is nothing more than a disappointment knowing what should have been but is not.

* * *

06/Aug/2020 06:06 PM

Deciding whether you like or dislike a creative project does not mean that you understand that creative project.

*　　*　　*
06/Aug/2020 09:59 AM

Are you pretending to be happy with where you find yourself in life or are you happy?

* * *
05/Aug/2020 03:18 PM

When was the last time you did something for someone you did not know and did not expect anything in return?

* * *
05/Aug/2020 03:06 PM

In life, you can generally never anticipate that the last time will be your last time.

High Tech Verses No Tech and the Art of Zen Filmmaking
04/Aug/2020 02:20 PM

As a filmmaker, I'm always exploring new ways to capture visual images in a unique and artistic manner. Though I tend to stay always from high tech gadgetry, since the birth of the iPhone I have used it to capture many images that made it into my *Zen Films*.

Though I was reluctant to do so, recently I purchased a very high-end gimbal thinking I could do so some interesting things with it. When I got it and started working with it, however, I realized that it had a mind of its own. Though it was suppose to respond certain ways to certain prompts, this was not always the case. It just got so frustrating. After a few days I discarded it.

A long while back, I had purchased this very simple pistol grip phone holder. I have used it many-many times all across the globe to capture footage. I realized that with it I could capture all that a gimbal could with a lot less frustration. I just had to do it manually. I made the joke to my lady, *"Just kept it Low Tech."* She chimed in, *"You mean No Tech."*

Here we reach one of the elemental rules of *Zen Filmmaking,* which is, *"Make the movie."* It doesn't matter how you get it done as long as you get it done.

Like I have now explained for decades, the reason so many people don't get their movies completed is because what they create never matches the mental vision of what they hoped to create. Thus, they never complete anything.

The reality of filmmaking, especially in the no-budget indie level, you must accept the obvious that without unlimited funds creating a movie on a small budget is going to be defined by what's available to you. This doesn't mean it can't look great. This doesn't man it can't be cinematic art. But, you have to be willing to accept and live with what you can get. Most would-be filmmakers are not willing to do this, however.

This brings me to another point. Obviously, *The Roller Blade Seven* is one of my most well known films. Commonly, people ask me will I ever make another one. Sometimes, even some of the actual cast members have contacted me, remembering what a wild crazy experience it was to be on that set, and wondering if they can be in the next one. This is all great! I am happy that people are still discovering that film and finding enjoyment in watching it. I am happy people still want to see the final chapter, as Donald G. Jackson and I originally planned to make it a trilogy. But, as I have also often said, the world has changed since we made RB7. There is just no way you could get that many people doing those kinds of things and film it for the amount of money that we filmed RB7. Look at the scope of that film. Stop judging the acting, the editing, and all that… Look at the visuals. Study them. To ever make something like that again would cost big-big money.

Sometimes people contact me and want to help me make another *Roller Blade Seven.* Of course, they're not offering to put up any money. They just want to be a part of something with that legacy. I get it. Again, that's great! I appreciate the asking. But, few ever look to what it takes to make a film with that magnitude actually happen.

For me, I've not made what could be considered a traditional, story-driven film in well over a decade. Artists evolve. Their art evolves. As an actor, I've worked on other people's films and was happy to do it. (Just to get in front of this, before anyone asks me to be in their indie film, I am an active member of SAG/Aftra, so I can only do union films). I've also done a bunch of commercials. I love it! It's all a lot of fun. But, as for what I create, I've moved into a different direction. Check out my *Zen Films* like *Mechanical Ballet, Transmundane Israel,* or *Streets: Los Angeles* on YouTube if you want to view what I'm into creating at this stage of my life. Plus, there's many more *Zen Films* on my YouTube channel if you really want to knock yourself out. They're all free. No ads! This is not to say that with the right inspiration I would not make another narrative film like RB7. But, the reality of the reality of making a film like that must be understood.

I am so happy that people still seek out my *Zen Films*. The ones created thirty years ago or yesterday. Even if they hate them, they have taken the time to view my interpretation of cinematic art at the various stages of my career. But, it is essential to understand that for each artist and their art form they are defined by availability. They make a choice about what they want to create and then they must find a way to actualize that creation.

At the heart of *Zen Filmmaking* is acceptance. Acceptance of your reality. Acceptance of who and what you have work with. And, acceptance of the ultimate truth of life that most things, in fact very few things, are going to turn out they way you have them envisions in your mind.

If you are free enough to accept the simplicity of reality, then anything you create become perfect in its own right. It becomes exactly what it should be. So, you can buy an expensive gimbal hoping to get some great shots with it if you want or you can grab a No Tech hand grip, slap your smart phone in it, and just get out there and film, creating cinematic art in the purest most simplest form possible.

Art is art. It doesn't matter how much it costs you to create it.

The Way of Initiation
04/Aug/2020 10:01 AM

The Sanskrit word, *"Dīkṣā,"* means, *"Initiation."* More precisely it refers to, *"Spiritual initiation."*

Initiation is the ceremony when a person who decides to become formally involved with a group or a spiritual sect is ceremoniously brought into the fold where the essential secrets and the metaphysical knowledge of the group may be revealed.

Many people, who have grown up in the western world, have been baptized into Christianity. This is a form of initiation. Though statistical evidence illustrates that these number have dropped over recent decades, many still have encountered that experience. In faiths such as Catholicism, this ceremony often times takes place when a person is an infant so it is not remember. Nonetheless, the ceremony was performed and the believers believe that a soul may be saved simply by that action.

As one moves forward through life, initiation becomes a much more conscious, personal decision. An individual deliberately chooses to become involved with a group, religious or otherwise, and then they choose to formally become a member of that group. Once they have partaken of the basic indoctrination they then may decide to become formally integrated into the group and this is where initiation takes place.

Initiation is a formal transmission where the adept accepts the novice into the assemblage. Though many people may be involved in the process as onlookers, initiation is defined by one person become a part of the greater whole.

Since the dawning of time there have been those who seek a higher knowledge. This knowledge is not solely limited to religious understandings. This knowledge may be academic, physical, or mental. But, what always occurs is that one person decides to learn and understand more and they do so by formally integrating themselves into a group.

Initiation is essential for any person to claim higher knowledge. Whether this higher knowledge is gained by going to school and earning a degree, going through martial art training and being awarded a belt rank, or by following a sanctified spiritual tradition and being formally initiated as a member, a person must proceed through the ranks and put in the time and then be certified as that something if they hope to be understood to hold true credentials in anything that they believe.

This is where the process of initiation has been bastardized in the modern era. With the dawning of technology, people began to learn subjects by mail. They began to study the martial arts, and other physical activates, via film and later videotape and now online. They began to read and memorize passages in books and claim the wisdom as their own. But, all of this does not involve initiation. It does not involve a person possessing the incentive to seek out a teacher, and then putting in the time and studying with that teacher, to truly learn a subject. Yes, a student can learn from books and from video presentations, but without a true basis in foundational knowledge all they will come away with is an eggshell of understanding. If a person is not given one-on-one instruction, having their subtle mistakes and misinterpretations corrected, they can never truly master an art; they can never truly know a subject. This is why formal initiation is absolutely necessary.

What is it that you want to know? What is it that you think you understand? Why do you want to know it? And, why do you believe you understand anything?

Anytime you encounter an individual who claims to be a knower of anything; you really need to inquire as to where it is that they received their foundational knowledge. For if they have not been awarded that degree, if they cannot tell you who they studied under, if they cannot tell you whom they were initiated by, then you must question as to whether or not the knowledge that they claim to hold is nothing more than something that they read in a book or picked up online.

Initiation is the transmission of essential wisdom. This is a required element in any pathway to higher knowledge. Though, once initiated, the student after a time of study may very well formalize their own credo, they can, nonetheless, point back to whom awarded them their foundational understanding. They can tell you whom they were initiated by.

All true knowledge begins with a basis of previously understood realizations. To truly actualize any self-originated anything, one must be able to point to whom they studied under and who initiated them into the pathway of advanced understanding.

Though you may think you know what you know; is that simply your ego speaking? If you cannot name your teachers in an established tradition, then all you are is a person who claims to be a knower with no foundational evidence.

Holding Me To My Past
03/Aug/2020 04:35 PM

I was planning to write a blog about, *"Aśeṣatā," "Parāvara,"* and *"Sākalya,"* the way a human brings together the various realms of life and of consciousness into one cohesively totality and merges them into the universal cosmic whole finding enlightenment. But, then I got a message from one of my on-line friends. They had come upon this old magazine somewhere where I am mentioned in an article. I had totally forgotten about that magazine and that article, but it peaked my interest. So, I went into the *Zen Filmmaking Archives* and pulled it out.

The main focus of the article was on one of my *Zen Filmmaking* partners—a great girl/a great person, who shall remain nameless. Reading it, I was reminded it was a total puff piece. It made me smile how the author of the article had (I guess) taken everything she had said, believed it, and wrote it down for the world to read as fact. She was making three movies a day, was posing for photographers, was writing articles for magazines, was teaching a class on photography at a local university, on and on… Wow. Think if you/think if anyone could do all that… I smiled…

It kind of got me to thinking about how so much that is out there is not really true. …Thinking about how people exaggerate.

Exaggeration is not really a bad thing; as long as it doesn't hurt anyone. And, it does create a mythical persona. But, the facts be the facts, it is not true.

Here she was this very successful person, yet she still stretched the truth about her reality.

When, think about it, how many women would have loved to live the life she was actually living?

Mostly, we were good friends back then. That article came out a long time ago but it was good to think of her, remember our filmmaking experiences, see some of the photos I took of her published in the pages of the magazine, and see our photos together.

As I was in the archives, I looked through a few other items. I came upon this photo of one of my *Zen Filmmaking* brothers. It was a photograph with him and his first wife. Looking at him, he was so young and they both looked so happy. That too made me smile. I guess forty years ago I was young too. ☺

Like my aforementioned friend, he too lived a very successful life. Me, I wasn't and still am not as successful as the either of them. But, the memories are good.

In my life, I have found that many people focus on my past. They still discuss movies I made thirty years ago, articles I wrote (or am mentioned in) a million years ago, books written way back in the way back when, you name it… There's also certain people that I lived a lot of life with, like my one buddy, who, whenever we get together all he does is fall back into a place of remembering what we did way back when. And, we did a lot. But really, what is the past? Is the past that place where you are young and beautiful and happy or is the past simply an illusion? Is it simply words written on the pages of a magazine that aren't really true?

Your reality is your reality. Just like mine is mine. For me, though I can obviously see the difference between who I was then and who I am now, when I look at old photographs, the me in the me has not changed. I am still the same person I always was. Physically older, yes. But, what is older? My mind has not aged. Who I am in my true mind/my consciousness has not gotten older at all.

Yes, a million life experiences have been live, leading me to where I find myself now. But, where I am internally is where I have always been. The only difference is the things that I do, and the people I associate with. But, those are just things. Things that make up memories. But, by the time you have lived those experiences that lead to those memories, you have already passed through them, so they cannot be lived again.

Any moment is gone as quickly as it can be experienced. If you don't make that moment matter, it does not matter.

How about you? Who were you way back when? Do you ever compare yourself? Sure, your life, your occupation, your responsibilities, the people you love, the people you hang out with may have all changed but have you changed? Again sure, you've grown up, you've gotten a better command over what you do and how you do it; how you interact with life and with others, but is the true inner you any different? Has who you are, deep down inside, changed?

Here's the really of life… We all live. We all have our experiences. We each are at times caused to look back through time. But, remembering yesterday's reality only leads us to where we are not. Sure, we may look back fondly at that period of time. We may remember our friends and it brings a smile to our faces. But, all we really have is right now. What we are doing at this moment, what we decided to do next, and what we create mentally as our pathway to human interaction unfolds.

You can remember the past if you want. You can lock yourself into what used to be. But, then is not now. If you don't make your now as full and fulfilled as possible you will have nothing to look back on tomorrow.

* * *

02/Aug/2020 03:47 PM

You can spend your entire life listening to the music someone else has created or you can go and create your own.

*   *   *
02/Aug/2020 03:46 PM

Even the oldest most broken down car was new once upon a time.

Do Something Good Today
01/Aug/2020 07:23 AM

When you woke up this morning what were you thinking about? Were you thinking about you? Were you thinking about someone else? Or, were you thinking about nothing?

When you woke up this morning what were you planning to do? Were you planning to do something for yourself? Were you planning to do something for something you have to do; like going to work? Or, were you planning to do something good for someone else expecting nothing in return?

Most people operate from a space of selfishness. Meaning, they only think about themselves and how what they do and what others do will affect them. How about you? What space of life-operations do you operate from? How often do you wake up with a consciousness plan to do something good for someone else or the entire world?

In life, we each possess the potential to do something good for someone else. In some cases, we can plan out these events and see them through to completion. In other cases, situations just come up where we see someone in need of some help and we help.

Doing good always equal something good. It helps someone and hurts no one. How often do you wake up in the morning and set about on a course of doing something good?

You know, your life is your life, your choices are your choices; you can make a decision to set your life on any course that you want. How often do you set about doing something good for someone?

Doing good is always good. It makes everyone involved feel better. Helping is always helpful. It makes everyone who needs help feel better.

So, what are you going to do today? Why don't you shift your mind from yourself: what you feel and what you want, and set about on a path of doing something good. Right now, set a course and do something good for someone. Do something good for someone you know. Do something good for someone you don't know.

Tomorrow morning, when you wake up, have a plan; possess a state of mind where you will not allow that day to be lived simply in a state of selfishness but instead be encountered with your mind knowing that you are going to do something good.

A better everything begins with you. Do something good today.

The Person Who Can't Grow a Conscience
31/Jul/2020 10:26 AM

Have you ever encountered a person that did something to hurt you but when you told them what they had done they did not care? Have you ever met a person who consciously set out to damage you or your life and when they had accomplished that act they took pride in their action?

As we pass through life we all encounter people of varying mental makeups. Some people are very nice, caring, and giving. Others are only in it for themselves. Still others, set about on a pathway that damages the life of one or more people and they do this without caring about the consequences to the life of the person they are impacting. Where do you find yourself in this assessment?

No one is perfect in life. We all make mistakes and we all do things that may unintentionally hurt someone else. Most people, however, when they do hurt someone else they apologize and try to fix or repair the damage that they created. Certainly, some people want some things from others that they simply cannot give. But, that is based in individual desire. That is not based in intentionally hurting. A person who targets and intentionally hurts someone simply because they can is a very specific type of individual.

When we look at life, I believe that we all can point to people who set about on a course to hurt someone else. Maybe that person who was hurt was you so you understand this dilemma very well. Maybe it was someone you cared about who was intentionally hurt by that someone else. Whatever the case, pain is pain, hurt is hurt, and anyone who knowingly hurts the life of someone else should be held accountable for the actions. But, are they? In many cases they are not.

The thing about life is that so much of it is defined by personal perspective. It is defined by how someone sees another person and experiences the actions they unleash. If you are close to a person, if you like a person, if you love a person, you may be very forgiving and seemingly understanding of their actions; even cheering on what someone does that hurts that someone else. The problem of this calculation is, however, if someone is hurt, someone is hurt. That person has taken the impact of the action. So, no matter how much you may like the person who unleashed that hurtful action, by reassuring them that what they did was okay, you become part of the greater karmic circle of that action even though you did not personally do it.

If you study the people who unleash negative actions onto others, you will witness that one thing is for sure; they do not do it to only one person. They do it to many. In fact, sometimes their mindset changes about a particular individual and someone who was once considered a friend becomes the objective of their attack. It is important to keep this in mind, as the next target may be you.

Most of us have a conscience. When we do something that hurts someone, it makes us feel bad and this motivates us to try to repair the damage we unleashed. Not everyone is like this, however. Some people knowingly hurt other people.

From the outside perspective, all of us who hope to live a conscious and good life know that this is not the type of individual we should associate with. But, not everyone hopes to live a conscious and a good life. Some enjoy the power felt by hurting others.

So, where does this leave us in life? I can say that we should all rebuke people who knowingly set about on a pathway of hurtful actions. But, life is complicated. Sometimes we must associate with those people. But, simply because we must associate with them does not mean that we have to be like them. We can be our own person and do all we can to make all life actions right, good, pure, and helpful.

Moreover, we each make a choice in life about who we are to become, the karma we are to create, and who we do or do not support as they live the life they choose to live. You can make a choice. You can do the right thing. You do not have to knowingly or unknowingly support the deviant deeds of a person who knowingly hurts others.

Being more starts with you. Being better starts with you. Doing good and helping others starts with you.

You are the impetus of change in all things life. Do the right thing. Hurt no one and never support the people that do.

* * *
30/Jul/2020 04:35 PM

Blaming is easy. It doesn't take any effort or ingenuity.

Life in the Time of Coronavirus
30/Jul/2020 01:38 PM

Unless you are a sadhu living in a cave in the Himalayas I doubt that there is anyone on this planet who has not been affected by the COVID-19 Coronavirus. Hundreds of thousands of people have died and millions have become sick. Others have gone broke and lost their businesses. This is a world catastrophe like one never seen before. Why? All because of an unregulated wet market in China.

Here in the U.S., we are currently in an election year. Politicians are attacking other politicians based on their response to the coronavirus. But, this is all just mind numbing rhetoric. It is all just people using this pandemic as a means and method to have something negative to say about someone else. The fact is, if they were in the position of power, making the decisions, they too would be criticized. Why? Because no one has the absolute answer as to what to do.

Months ago, when this pandemic was first taking hold/taking control over the world, I questioned in this blog and elsewhere, why is no one angry at China? This is their fault. And, I still raise this question.

As I also stated months ago, for the conspiracy theorists, maybe China did this on purpose. Maybe it was unleashed from that biochemical lab in Wuhan as some have suggested. Think about it, before this pandemic there were daily and nightly demonstrations and riots in Hong Kong about China's attempt to enact a law that allowed them to transport anyone they felt was doing things against the government to the mainland for trial. With the onset of the pandemic, all of the protests stopped. Now, they have enacted that law. In fact, just today, they removed all of the opposition candidates from Hong Kong's parliamentary elections. Why? Because they can. The opinions of the population of Hong Kong and the others countries around the world be damned.

Like I also said, in the blog from months past, I have had a lot of personal interactions in China, with the people and the government: both good and bad. Ever since I first traveled there, decades ago, I knew they would become a major world power—perhaps the greatest world power. Why? Because they have a massive population that is scared to death of the government. Again, why? Because of the way they manhandle their people. Just look at what they have done to their ethnic populations and to their dissidents. Look what they have done to Tibet. And, look out Taiwan.

China is a fact of life. This pandemic is a fact of life. And, due to a wet market (or a lab) in China think how many lives have been destroyed by something that emerged from China. Think how much saddest there is across the globe due to the loss of life of loved ones and to the loss of the livelihoods of so many. The repercussions of this pandemic will be felt for a very-very-very long time.

So again, why is no one mad at China? Why are we focusing our energy on blaming our own politicians, and our own people, solely as a means to vet our anger or to drive home our political ideology? We should not be mad at each other, we should be angry with China.

Like the lyric in the great song from the 1968 cult movie classic, *Wild in the Streets,* says, *"Nothing can change the shape of things to come."*

Performed by the fictional band, Max Frost and the Troopers, this song has become the truth. China is in control of the world. And, as they have proven, no one can change what they have unleashed.

China, what they did and/or did not do, has come to take control over the entire planet. Why is no one expressing their anger at China?

* * *
30/Jul/2020 09:23 AM

How much of what matters to you matters to anybody else?

Everybody Wants a Free Lunch
29/Jul/2020 09:04 AM

Everybody wants a free lunch AKA what you bring to the table verse what you take away…

Think about your life. Where do you find yourself in terms of your progression? Where do you find yourself in terms of where you want to be? Where do you find yourself in terms of who you want to be? Where do you find yourself now compared to where you believed that you would be five years ago?

Life is a pathway of desires and accomplishments. Some desires are locked solely in your mind. Others, you desire and you try to achieve. Certainly, as the Buddha so perfectly stated, *"The cause of suffering is desire."* But, this does not change the fact of the equation that people want what they want. What do you want? What did you want? What did and what do you do to get that something?

In many cases, people find themselves locked into a life trajectory that they cannot escape. So, they lived a knowingly unfulfilled life forever. Most are not like that, however. They at least try to get what they want.

Like I always say, *"Everybody wants to be a movie star."* But, for most this is the impossible dream so the majority of people do not even try. This does not take away their desire, however. And, this is where the problems of desire are laid. Just because you do not attempt to achieve your desire does not mean that you do not have that desire.

How many desires involve other people? Meaning, of your desires, how many of them require other people to be involved?

The reason I ask this question, and the reason you should define this fact in your mind, is that the moment other people are required to achieve your desire the entire playing field is changed as that other person/those other people need to be willing to play a part in your desire. If they don't, they don't. Then what?

How many times in your life have you approached other people asking them to help you achieve your desire? What was their response?

The thing is, most people want a free lunch. They want to do to that something, they hope to achieve that something, and they want/expect it to be given to them for free. Some even hope to be paid by some other person as they achieve that desire of their dreams.

In the world of cinema, this is so often the case. Though a person desires to be an actor, and they may be willing to pay for acting classes and the like, the moment they have the chance to step in front of the camera they want to be paid. But, isn't being given the chance to be in a movie payment enough? (How few are the people who are ever offered a chance to be in a movie?) This is why so many actors never get far in the pursuit of their desire; they want to be paid to live their dream.

This is a similar situation to people who hope to make money off of the creative cinema of someone else. Why do distributors contact a filmmaker? They contact them because they know they have a finished product and they understand, because that product is finished, they can sell it and make money off of it. But, they didn't envision the film. They didn't create that film. They didn't pay for that film to be created. Yet, they hope to make money off of that movie. Like I always say when presented with one of these situations, *"Go make your own movie."*

Now, filmmaking is just one aspect in the process of desire. Most people hold desires for many other things.

Think about your own desires. Take a moment and make a mental list of them. What do you want right now? Clearly define that something in your mind. What will it take for you to achieve that something? And, are you willing to do it?

Once this is clearly defined in your mind, really work this out. Follow the pathway of achieving your desire in your mind. What can you do? What are you willing to do? What can you do to make your desire a reality? But, more than all this, is your desire even haveable? Is there any way that you can actually make it happen? Be honest with yourself. Can you achieve what you dream of achieving and what will it cost to make that desire a reality?

Most people never plot a clear pathway to the achievement of their desires. They never calculate the, *"Other person,"* that it will take to make their dreams come true. They never take that person truly into consideration and because of this fact they are often let down because the other person is not willing to buy them lunch.

Because most people do not truly take that, *"Other person,"* into consideration, when they are turned down by that person they either become angry with that individual or hurt by that person. Then, all kinds of karma-latent activities are given birth to, causing a person to move farther away from the achievement of their desire.

So, let's go back to the beginning. What do you desire? Who else, besides you, is required to achieve that dream? Is that other person or persons willing to participate? And, are you seeking a free lunch? Are you taking something from somebody? Are you looking for someone to give you something so you can get—so you can achieve what you hope to achieve?

If you looking for a free lunch, if getting what you want means someone else has to buy it for you, the fact is, you will probably not achieve your desire.

True life/living a good life, involves what you bring to the table verses what you take away. What do you have to offer in the fulfillment of your desire?

It's Not the Color of Your Skin
It's the Kind of Person That You Are
28/Jul/2020 10:06 AM

There is a lot of talk about racism, racial profiling, and racial inequality going around these days. Certainly, racism is everywhere, practiced by every culture on earth. We may wish that were not the case, but that is a fact of life.

In most cultures across the globe, various ethnicities, have encountered prejudice based upon their race. It does not matter if you are a Caucasian, of African origin, of Asian origin, of Indigenous origin, of whatever origin, depending upon where you find yourself on the globe, you may encounter racism.

Some people sadly define every person they meet simply by their race. But, they are truly missing the point about humanity if this is the practice that they practice. A person's race is not the definition of who and what they truly are. How a person behaves towards other people and life is the definition of who and what they truly are.

I've had a few very interesting, telling experiences over the past couple of weeks that ideal illustrates how a person's behavior defines who they are, how the encounter life, and how what they do will come to define how other people will define them.

I was about to park my car in a corner parking spot the other day at the supermarket. Just as I was pulling into the spot this middle-aged Caucasian lady literally pushed her empty shopping cart right in front of my car, leaving it right in the middle of the parking spot. She turned and walked away not even thinking about what she had done. I had to get out of my car and move the shopping cart so that I could park in that spot. I did this, while she got into the passage seat of her car and her husband drove away not even taking note of my glaring stare.

About two weeks ago I was driving through this very narrow street in an affluent neighborhood. I come upon this SUV. Kind of like you might see in a comedy movie or a Sitcom there was this guy with his legs on the ground but his head and body were buried deep inside the car. What he was apparently doing was cleaning out his car as he was throwing all his trash out onto the street over his shoulder. My first thought was, *"Who does that?"* But, as this was such a narrow passageway I gave him a little honk just to let him know that there was a car approaching and not to throw his trash at me. As it turns out, he was an African American man who had his head buried in the car. He stands up and glares at me. I have seen this, *"Thug life,"* look so many times before; like he was a total badass and I better watch out. I smiled and nodded at him. I drive on. As I did, he does one of those hard spits on the ground as I pass like some sort of a warning. That made me smile.

The other day I was doing a fast-paced cardio walk with my lady through our neighborhood. As we come up to this side street this SUV barrels into the intersection. An Asian woman drove the car. She was doing that thing that so many bad, uncaring drivers do, simply assuming that there would be nobody walking through the intersection so she far overshoots the stop sign and the line that is painted into the street and has to skid to a stop to not hit us. I stopped quickly in my tracks to keep from being hit and throw up my arms. She looks at me and gives me one of those, *"Fuck off,"* hand waves, like this situation was somehow my fault.

I was having breakfast this morning at a restaurant. For the record, this piece is being written while we are at the height of the COVID-19 Coronavirus Pandemic, so, at least here in California, restaurants are only allowed to serve customers outside. In any case, my lady and I were eating and this elderly old white guy decides he needs a lime for his water. He goes up to the container holding the limes and sticks his hand in there, grabbing several but taking only one. Does this unthinking asshole not consider that this is how COVID-19 can be spread and what he just did, based upon something he couldn't wait a few minutes for the server to properly do for him, may end up costing somebody their life?

In each of those cases, an individual of a different race performed these actions. Were any of these actions based upon race? Did they do what they did defined by their race? Maybe, I don't know? But, what I do know is that is not even the point. In any of those situations what was done was done by one person choosing to invoke an action that had the potential to hurt someone or to cause another person to negatively react. Any of those situations could have resulted in a fight. And, that is what makes those people doing those things the person in the wrong. It has nothing to do with their ethnicity.

If we look across the U.S. right now, a lot of people are out there protesting. Sure, there's the anarchists out there simply destroying to destroy, but more than not, most of the people protesting are attempting to instigate change based upon what they believe is a society that has been developed upon racism. But, race does not matter unless you make it matter—unless you allow it to matter. What matter is what a person does and how they choose to interact with other people and with the world around them. Sure, you can define an individual's action based upon their race. But, at the end of the day all that matters is what a person (of whatever race) does. What matter is how they treat and react to other people.

Goodness is brought into this world via doing good things. Badness is brought into this world by people not taking the other person into consideration and simply doing what they do based upon their own level of self-entitlement and arrogance. If you're White, if you're Black, if you're Asian is all you are defined by your race? Is all you are how others define you by your race? Or, are you what you choose to be and what you decide to do?

Envisioning good always instigates the higher good. Are you going to allow others to define you by your race and keep you from embracing the higher good? Are you going to believe you are better than someone else simply because of your race, which will keep you from embracing the higher good? Or, are you going to do good things, say good things, see everyone for who they truly are and not create adversarial situations, thereby creating a world where everyone has the potential to be all they can be and do all the good that they can do. It all begins with you.

*   *   *
27/Jul/2020 07:18 AM

If you define your life by the mistakes you've made you have no chance of ever achieving any level of excellence.

*　　*　　*
26/Jul/2020 05:15 PM

Enlightenment is not the ending it is only the beginning.

* * *

26/Jul/2020 07:50 AM

What happens when you do something wrong in heaven?

What Do You Like To Do?
24/Jul/2020 07:38 AM

What do you like to do? For each of us it is different but we each have things that we enjoy doing. What is yours?

Sure, we all also have things we don't like to do. Sometimes those things are brought more clearly into focus in our lives because when we are doing them, we really hate the doing. But, lets focus on what you like to do.

What do you like to do? It can be more than one thing. Take a moment and really define and focus on the thing(s) you like to do. Define them in your mind. These things can be big or they can be small. But, whatever they are focus on the things you really enjoy doing.

For me, I like to make coffee in the morning. I certainly understand that is a very small thing. But, I enjoy doing it so, when I do it, I do it with conscious enjoyment each day.

And, this is the point, most people do not focus on the things they like to do. Even though they enjoy doing them, they think very little about the doing. Thus, their doing becomes lost into the nothingness of each of our lives. Those moments do not become remembered or embellished. They do not become our meditation. And, that is wrong.

As is well illustrated via techniques like Chanoyu, (commonly known as the Japanese Tea Ceremony), anything you do can become a meditation. It can become a pathway to some greater something. You simply have to perform it as such.

So, take a moment right now, define the thing(s) that you really like to do. Consciously come to understand how they make you feel when you are doing them. And, from this point forward, when you are doing them, stop your racing mind from making them just a task and truly immerse yourself in the doing while you are doing; make it memorable, make it a meditation of happiness.

*   *   *

23/Jul/2020 10:49 AM

Is a soldier better than a yogi? Or is a yogi better than a soldier?

Are You Locked In To Who You Used To Be?
23/Jul/2020 10:48 AM

In life, most people evolve. They become new and different versions of themselves. This is not to say that people always become better versions of themselves. But, they assuredly become different versions.

Most people, as they pass through life, hope to become better. They hope to progress, advance, learn, change and become the best version of themselves that they can be. Others follow a dark pathway and they become lost in bad behavior or mean-spirited, vengeful actions. Perhaps they become locked into following a hate culture or become lost in addition. But, in very few cases, as a person progresses through their years, do they remain the same.

Some people do some very bad things. By doing these bad things their entire life destiny becomes defined by those actions. From these bad actions, the person's life and who they did those bad actions to also becomes defined by that person's deeds. Of course, that is very sad.

In some cases, these people strive to repair and repay the actions they committed. In other cases, some people are surrounded by those who hail their bad deeds. Or, they are simply too locked into their own sense of self-definition and denial that they do not allow themselves to become aware of the pain that they have caused and thus they become locked into the person who did those bad deeds forever. From this, they become bound by a stagnate state of life evolution forever. How about you? Where do you find yourself in this life equation?

Most people, try to do good things. Most people, never desire to hurt anyone. Most people, if they do set a life course for themselves, do so as a means to give and give back to other people. They hope to learn and grow and care and give. How about you? Where do you find yourself in this life equation?

Many people live in a state of undefined self-reality. They simply do what they do in life, defined by what they are offered, and never truly study who and what they actually are and/or who they truly should become.

Some find a pathway to success and from that positioning they live in a state of oblivion, believing themselves to be living a good life simply because they are able to own what they want and to control their environment to the degree that can hold self-pride. Again, how about you? Where do you find yourself in this life equation?

Many people strive throughout their life to become more. This, *"More,"* takes the form of many definitions described uniquely by the individual mind. But, what is, *"More?"* Is, *"More,"* you owning more? Is, *"More,"* you doing more? Is, *"More,"* you controlling more? Or, is, *"More,"* you giving more?

How much of your life have you spent consciously trying to evolve into becoming a better person? How much of your life have you spend righting your wrongs? How much of your life have you spent finding a way to help others? Or, has your only pathway to life evolution focused on you: what you have, what you own, and how you are perceived by those around you and the greater world as a whole?

We all change as we pass through life. Most life change is not a path of conscious evolution, however. It is simply a path of forced realization. You are given what you are given and then you make the most of it.

The thing is, true life evolution is not based upon acquisition. It is based upon emancipation. It is based upon you freeing yourself from any negative deeds you have done, any adverse thoughts you think, any harmful actions you are planning, and moving forward into a space of enlightened life interaction.

Take a moment; define how you have evolved in the past ten years, one year, one month. Look to who you used to be and define what you have become. Was your evolution a consciousness process or did it just happen? How much of a participant were you in your life evolution?

Now, ask yourself, what do you want to become? Where do you want to be, what do you want to be doing: tomorrow, next week, next year? And, how can you get there?

Tomorrow starts with today. Today is based upon what you did yesterday. Who were you yesterday? Did you own, did you repair your yesterday, if it needed repairing? Did you set your destiny then for what you became today? And, what are you living today that will ideally create your tomorrow?

Take the time to consciously evolve.

Charting Your Arrogance
21/Jul/2020 09:45 AM

"Auddhayta," is the Sanskrit word for arrogance. It is one of those wide-spanning words that can be translated into various forms of arrogance including: arrogant behavior, self-exaltation, distain for others, self-superiority, overbearing behavior, and vanity. No matter how a person exhibits arrogance, or by what name you define it, arrogance is arrogance and though many people thrive, at least for a time, within its realms, it is a very damaging emotional exhibition not only to the people it is unleashed upon but to the arrogant person themselves.

Think about your life. Think about the people you have encountered who were arrogant. How did their arrogance dominate their interpersonal interactions? How did it come to define them as a person? Were they ultimately liked? Or, did their behavior damage others while they basked in their own self-defined superiority?

Most people who exist in a space of arrogance are not self-aware enough to admit to themselves that they are arrogant. They are simply so full of themselves, and what ever it is they may or may not have accomplished, that they become lost in their own self-righteousness.

Others, who exist in the realms of arrogance, do so very knowingly. As they are behaving in the manner they are behaving, with a consciousness of their actions, some even pretend that they are not arrogant at all. They do it with a smile on their face.

No matter how an arrogant person exhibits and portrays their arrogance, they, nonetheless, exist in a world where they feel they are better than someone/anyone. With this, they cast their self-definition onto all of their relationship.

Have you met an arrogant person? Most of us have. Have you ever portrayed arrogance? Most of us, at some point in our lives, have felt very proud of something we have done or something we have become and we were less than humble. Though perhaps this arrogance lasted only for a moment, most of us have experienced it in our lives.

Some people pursue a position of arrogance. They enter into a livelihood or a life style that embellishes arrogance. Certainly, in fields like the martial arts you will find arrogant people all the time based in their belief that they can fight better than the average person or that they hold some advance black belt rank making them more than all of their juniors.

I think back to a time many years ago when I was out having a beer with this one very famous martial artist and a few other Korean masters. He's still around today. Anyway, as can be the case in bars, somebody said something rude to him and him, in all his arrogance, (he was really an arrogant guy), got confrontational. I'm sure he believed he held the advantage. In an instant this other guy handed him his ass, however. The Korean, *"Master,"* was on the ground all but knocked out. This all happened before any of us, or anyone, could break up the fight.

This is a very good example of arrogance—a person believing they are better than other people simply because they are self-indoctrinated to believe that they are. This is also why I long ago realized that it doesn't matter what black belt rank you hold in a street fight as a hardened street fighter holds all the cards in those situations. Like I always say, *"Rank is just a name and a number on a piece of paper."* Yet, throughout the martial arts people seek and hold rank and base their entire life, life style, occupation, and arrogance on the name and the number on that piece of paper.

Certainly, successful people from all fields exhibit arrogance. They thrive on their accomplishment(s). They thrive on the way people look up to them. They thrive on the way people want something from them. They thrive on the way they can get people to give them what they want. But, what does any of that mean? What does it do for the person? What does it do for the greater good?

Arrogance is arrogance no matter what is its source. Self-pride is self-pride. But, what does that do for anything?

The fact of the matter is, as human beings we are taught to strive for accomplishment. We are schooled to believe that we want to be close to and gain from those who are accomplished. Thus, we all, if we follow that pathway, give birth to a person's arrogance.

But, a person can be successful and be humble. A person can be accomplished and be caring. A person can be certified and awarded and still can care more about the other person than him or her self.

Like I say over and over again, all life begins with you. It begins with what you do. It begins with how you behave. A person does not need to choose to be arrogant. And yes, arrogance is a choice.

So, who are you? Are you arrogant? Are you arrogant and pretend not to be? Are you basing your life on what you have accomplished? Or, are you basing your life upon what you have given to others and to the greater good?

If you look at yourself as a something, you are arrogant. If you look at yourself as nothing, you are free. Free to care more about others than yourself. From this space in life you can truly give, you can truly care, you can truly make the all and the everything just a little bit better.

Let go of arrogance. Let go of worshiping the arrogant.

*   *   *

20/Jul/2020 03:08 PM

If you hurt someone you will always be remembered as the person who hurt them.

If you help someone you will always be remembered as the person who helped them.

Looking Too Deeply for Something That Isn't There
20/Jul/2020 01:59 PM

It seems that it is a trait of human nature that some people wish to put their definition onto anything that is created outside of themselves. I am not speaking about the artists here, for they are at the creative sourcepoint for anything that they create. They know what they are talking about. But, I will get to that in a moment. What I am speaking about is the way some people wish to interpret the something of someone else and cast their own interpretation/their own judgment onto it.

Think about it, how many interpretations of the Bible, the Koran, the Bhagavad Gita, the Dharmapada, the Tao Te Ching have there been throughout the centuries? Each interpreted in the way the interpreter wished the scriptures to be understood.

If you take this interpenetrative ideology onto all things scriptural, technological, art, or anything created or done by someone else, the number of interpretations at the hands of someone else is unfathomable. Yet, think how many people read or listen to these interpretations. More people read or listen to someone else's interpretation than go to the source and study the material themselves.

They commonly do this thing in art schools where they have the other students in a class evaluated the creations of their fellow students. Sometimes these critiques are very harsh. But, what they all are, for sure, is self-motivated. Each student is basing their critiques on their own personal bias. They are saying what they say based upon what they feel about the artwork and/or the other student.

But, all of that is based in Self, not in true absolute knowledge. If you look, if you listen, you will always find the personality of the person in what they say. This is why in the classes that I teach I never allow this style of evaluation to take place. For how can anyone ever truly understand the art created by someone else?

From my own personal perspective, I have read or listened to people's interpretations, critiques, and criticisms of my writings and my art, (cinematic and otherwise), since I began creating. In some cases, some people, have created elaborate presentations: documented writings, videos, podcasts, you name it. Some are good. Some are bad. Some are very attack orientated and self-serving. Others are fun or funny. But, the one thing that none of them are is accurate. In every single case, whether the pieces was based on positivity or negativity, they were not the person who created the art so they completely got the motivations, the activations, the process, and the reason why completely wrong.

Look around the internet, you can find all kinds of reviews and presentations about my writings and my films all over the place. There have even been some elaborately created pieces about my very obscure films. Read them, listen to them, and all you will see or hear is a person's interpretation of what I have created. But, they're not me. They weren't part of the process. They weren't around when I was writing the book or creating the film. So, all you will read or hear is what they think about what I have done based upon their own personal bias. ...A person, who was not involved in the creation, telling other people what they think about what someone else has done. Is that art?

This is the same for every review ever written. I'm just using myself as an example here, as I know some of the stuff that has gone on. But, think about it; look around, how many people have something to say about what someone else has done? Do you?

In life, we all come to like what we like and dislike what we dislike. I'm no different. But, what I do not do is to cast my judgment onto what someone else has created in a manner that is based in my own self-motivated, self-defined interpretation of that creation. I allow the artist to be the artist and to create what they create. If I like it, great! If I don't, great! What I do not do is to try to describe what they have done or detail their inspirations, motivations, or critique the outcome based upon my interpretation.

You can go through life loving or hating anything. You can go through life telling people what you think about what someone else has created. But, if you do this, you are admitting to the world that you are wrong. Because you are talking/you are writing about something that you truly do not understand. You weren't there when the work was created. You probably do not personally know the artist. Thus, you have no factual basis for anything that you write or you say. All you have is your interpretation that is based in nothing more than your own personal bias.

Be more than a review. Become the artist.

The Contact of the Creative Contractual
20/Jul/2020 08:11 AM

Recently, a friend of mine had hooked up with a guy and they set about making a movie about skateboarders. They had gotten fairly well into it when he contacted me, as they needed the interview segments for the film. As he didn't own a camera or a microphone and really didn't have the understanding about how to light the scenes, etc., he asked if I would come on board and help him out. *"Sure."* We got a location. I filmed the stuff for him and that was that.

The other day, he gave me a copy of the film to watch. I sat down to watch it and the first thing I noticed about it was the main player in the game had put in all these very small, very extensive front end credits, kind of like the kind you may see in the end credits. He even put his address in the front end credits. Anybody watching it, who actually wanted to read all that was there, would have to stop the movie. I watched a couple of minutes of it but as I didn't see my name in the credits and as I tend to be an impatient person, especially when it comes to low budget homegrown indie films, I just turned it off. I mean, I had just watched the new Tom Hanks film, Greyhound, which was a great movie. I was not in the mood for slow paced boredom.

A couple of days later my friend asked me if I would sit down and watch the movie with him. I reluctantly agreed. After sitting through it with him I realized that the main player/editor had not used any of the footage we had shot. All that was presented was a fairly standard/fairly boring visual presentation with no punch or reasoning for why it was a movie. My friend was very upset the guy had not used our footage and wanted to confront the guy and asked if I would go along. I knew this was probably going to turn into a mess but I agreed.

The main player was one of those young film school grads that thinks he knows it all, has the world by the tail, and is going to break big ASAP. I've met so many of them. Where are they now???

Anyway, his explanation for not using the footage was, he didn't want anyone else's hand in the film; i.e. mine. Sure, I get it. I questioned in my mind why did he ask his partner, my friend, to get the footage in the first place but whatever… I was helping out my friend and if something came of it, great. If not, it didn't change the experience.

My friend, however, was pissed. And, they started going back and forth. I suggested that the main guy just give my friend the footage we shot and let bygones be bygones. He refused to give up the footage, however. And. it all ended with a bunch of screaming, *"I am going to sue you!"*

I know people throw those words around a lot, but what few understand is that suing someone is very-very expensive. It ain't free. So, unless you've got the finance behind you to do that, it rarely happens.

The reason I tell this story is that it goes to the essence of life and creativity. Some people want to create. The problem is, there are generally other people involved in the equation and that is where the problems begin.

Personally, I've worked on movies, as an actor, which never found their way to daylight. Some were highly financed. Why? I don't know? Of course, I would have liked to see them. But, there was nothing I could do.

As a filmmaker, I made movies where I've had to cut people's scenes out of the final cut. A couple of times I was really sorry I had to do that but it was more based in the composition of the scene than their acting. Especially back in the day, when you never really knew what you had filmed until you were done. Sometimes the cameraman fucked up or the quality of the scene just wasn't there and the scene would not have passed quality control for international distribution. In other words, shit happens. And, you've got to be prepared for it.

The other side of the issue is people—the people you work with. If you are working with someone with a big ego or a person who wants to control the everything you are more then likely going to run into problems as did my friend. But, what can you do if you enter into one of those situations? …Get mad, fight, or just follow the path of least resistance and understand that some people are just selfish assholes?

After we left the confrontational discussion, my friend was obviously upset. What would become of the movie? I don't know? He didn't know. Personally, I had no horse in the race so I didn't really care. But, obviously my friend did. And, this is the reality of life; it generally takes more than one person to do that creative something, like a movie, but no matter what, there always has to be one person in the driver's seat. Otherwise, everything just becomes convoluted. It you're the one riding shotgun, you have to just take that ride and be accepting of the outcome. If you're the one driving, you're in control but you're probably going to make an enemy or two along the way. That's just reality—creative reality.

In this world, creating movies has become so easy. All you need is the mental focus and a smart phone. But, there is also so much more out there these days to easily create movies in a specular fashion. What I suggested to my friend was that he get a couple of GoPros, strap them onto the skateboards of some of the skaters he already had met, get them reinterviewed, and make a better movie than he was already involved with creating. *"It's easy to do,"* I exclaimed.

He asked me if I would produce it for him. I said, *"No thanks."* ☺

The thing is, if you want to create, create. Get out there and do it. There is so much bad stuff having already been done, yours can't be any worse. And besides, good or bad should never be entered into the equation. The only thing that you should care about is that you have the mental focus to get that project done.

Like I always say, start small. Get your phone, film some stuff, and tie it all together. Whether it is one minute or thirty minutes it doesn't even matter. Length doesn't matter. All that matters is that you have a made a film.

Don't get lost in the process. Don't get lost in the ego. Don't get lost in the good or the bad. Simply create!

*   *   *

19/Jul/2020 09:06 AM

The person who steals from others always screams the loudest when something is stolen from them.

The person who hurts others always screams the loudest when they are hurt.

The person who lies always screams the loudest when they are lied to.

The person who judges others always screams the loudest when they are judged.

The person who criticizes others always screams the loudest when they are criticized.

The person who is deceitful always screams the loudest in an attempt to protect the truth about who and what they truly are.

The person who is vain always screams the loudest when their beauty is challenged.

The person who believes they are right always screams the loudest when they are proven to be wrong.

The person who is good, caring, and giving is silent.

* * *
17/Jul/2020 03:14 PM

Do you ever question why a person wants to hurt another person?

* * *
17/Jul/2020 07:28 AM

You may want somebody to care about you but if they don't there's nothing you can do to change their mind.

What You Should Be Doing is Apologizing
16/Jul/2020 04:39 PM

Have you ever been in one of those situations where somebody doesn't like you or somebody becomes mad at you so they say and do things in an attempt to hurt your life? Most of us have encountered this type of a life situation in one form or another. If you ever watch Reality TV, this kind of behavior goes on all the time. It is situations like that, where it is broadcast like a soap opera, you can really see into the self-motivated intentions of people. Like the old saying goes, *"With friends like that who needs enemies?"*

On the personal level, when somebody decides to target you, his or her actions can be very devastating. And, that is assuredly what they hoped for. They want to hurt you. But, why do they want to hurt you? No matter what you did or did not do to them, the reason they want to hurt you is all based in their own mind. It is based upon what they feel is right or what they feel is wrong. It is how they see you in relation to their own life. But, if you study that equation, all it is actually based upon is what they are thinking and what they are feeling. Thus, whenever they act upon those emotions, all they are doing is casting their judgment onto you and moving it outwards onto the world.

Of course, on the internet this kind of stuff is everywhere. Why? Because everybody is nobody. They are an illusional character. Even if they use their own true name and their own true face, which most people do not, they are nothing more than an emoji or a meme. Yet, no matter where or how this person instigates their attack, they are basing their entire ideology on themselves, they are never taking your point of view into consideration and, thus, they are doing what they are doing based upon a very low level of psychological evolution.

If you look at the world today, in recent times, there have been a lot of people crying out for justice. Whether it is the #metoo movement, #blm, #alllivesmatter, you name it, it is all based upon people doing bad things to other people and the people who were hurt hoping for and wanting repayment for the damages that were created by the hands of others.

But, look at life, bad behavior is all around us all the time and, in some cases, people are even praised for it. Every time a person smokes and makes other people breathe in their second hand smoke, they are doing damage to the lives of other people. #icantbreathe Every time some unthinking person does not wear a facemask when they encounter other people, in this age of COVID-19 coronavirus, they are potentially killing someone simply because they feel they have the right not to wear a mask. But do they? Does anyone actually have the right to hurt anyone else simply because they do not take that other person's feelings, that other person's rights, that other person's physical or mental health, or that other person's life into consideration?

Think about the people that have knowingly set about to hurt your life. Did they ever apologize? If they did not, how did that make you feel?

Think about the people that you have knowing set about hurting? Did you ever apologize? How do you feel about that? Do you ever even think about that? Or, are you so locked into your own sense of judgment, your own sense of self-worth, your own sense of self-image that you feel you have the right to say and do whatever it is you feel like saying or doing no matter what it does to the life of someone else?

Hurting, is the lowest level of human evolution. Unhurting is the highest.

What are you going to do about what others have done to you? Are you going to learn for the damage inflicted onto your life and never do that damage to anyone else?

What are you going to do about what you have said and done that has hurt the life of other people? Are you going to apologize and try to right the wrong?

You can answer those questions any way you want. You can choose to response to those questions in any manner that you want. You can turn things around and try to blame someone else for what you have done. But, if you step back from your own self-involved mindset, based in judgment, we all know what you should do.

Apologize.

* * *
16/Jul/2020 08:07 AM

What have you taken from someone else that you never gave them credit for?

* * *
16/Jul/2020 08:07 AM

We all have something to cry about.

*   *   *
15/Jul/2020 01:29 PM

What do they do to have fun in heaven?

The Things Your Didn't Do
15/Jul/2020 10:03 AM

Exercise for the day:

Right now, take a moment and think about the things you did not do. …The things in life that you knew you should have done but for whatever reason you did not do them.

To better understand the concept of this exercise, it is not focused on the little things you should have done, like asking that person for their phone number or buying that pair of shoes that you really liked but when you returned to the store they were gone. This exercise is based in the big things you should have done that you did not do. For example: going to college, getting a degree, studying yoga, learning the martial arts, learning how to play guitar, learning how to paint, studying how to write, learning a new language, climbing that mountain to its summit, to stop smoking, to stop drinking, to stop taking drugs. The big things that now, as you look back, you regret not doing.

In each of our lives there is a point of flux. There are substantial moments that come and then they go. It is in that moment where we make our decisions, based upon any number of variables, and that choice comes to be a defining factor in our lives. The older you get, the more of these points of flux exist. But, no matter what age you are, there is a moment where you made a choice and that choice changed the evolution of your future. What is that moment/what was that choice for you?

As stated, the older you get the more flux points you have. But, for each of us there are very specific moments that stand out in our brain where the choices we made, in that moment, come to be a defining factor of our lives. Isolate one of those moments in you. Bring it clearly into focus. What was it? When was it? Why did you make the choice to not do that something? And, how did that choice affect your life? How did it affect it then? How is it affecting it right now?

There is nothing you can do in life to change the choices you made in the past. In some cases, however, you can pick up where you left off many years ago. Situations like this are illustrated when the older adult goes back to school and things like that. Ask yourself, can you do now what you decided not to do then? If you can, why don't you do it? If you can't, why can't you?

Each of our lives is made up by the choices we make. In each of our lives we later realize that we should have done something differently. For some, this becomes the defining factor of their life. From this, they regret and they blame. But, all of that does nothing to change what is missing from your life by the choices you have made.

Most people never do anything about the wrong choices they made. For some, they never possess the opportunity to make anything any better. This may be due to finances, family commitments, or work responsibilities. For others, they simply do not try. What is the reason you have not attempted to rethink your original choice when you know you should have made a separate decision? What are you doing now that is keeping you from remaking that choice?

Life is based upon what you choose to do. All of the choices of all of our lives are based upon a combination of personal decisions and life determinates that we have little or no control over.

The more you relinquish control, the less control you ultimate possess. This is particularly the case when you are an adult and you are the person who can truly control your life if you choose to.

What was that thing or things you should have done? Why can't you do it/them now?

If you want something in your life there is only one way to get it. That one way is to try. You may try and you may fail, but if you do not try you can never know what the having of that something will feel like.

Look at the flux point of your life. Do you still want that something? If you do, try to obtain it.

Wisdom
14/Jul/2020 09:22 AM

"Chitta," "Dhirata," "Buddhimatta." These words, translated from Sanskrit, all refer to, *"Wisdom."*

As I always say, whenever I reference a word in Sanskrit, when you take a word from an ancient dialect, and move it to a modern language, sometimes some of the subtitles of the true meaning of the word are lost. This being said, we all can understand the meaning of the word, *"Wisdom."*

When one follows the eastern tradition of spirituality, as they progress through the ranks (so to speak) they are often given a new name. This name generally is in Sanskrit. The reason a new name is provided is so that the individual has a reminder that they have left their old life behind and that they have emerged as a new and different person. The changing of the name is a tool.

I have known people that were provided with a name referencing wisdom. The name also can provide the individual with something to focus upon as they progress through their spiritual evolution.

Wisdom is an important thing. It is we, as a person, as a people, moving towards a higher understanding of not only ourselves but of life, reality, and god.

Sometimes some people find their way to wisdom simply by living life experiences. Sometime some people are forced into encountering wisdom due to living through a certain life experience. Sometimes some people actually seek it out and truly try to raise their life understanding and consciousness. Most, however, do none of the above. This is what makes wisdom a truly unique entity onto itself.

Think about the people you believe are wise. Why is that? Why do you believe that they are wise? What qualities do they exhibit that makes you believe they are wise? Have you actually met that person? Have you encountered their wisdom firsthand?

Wisdom is an overreaching concept that transcends the limitation of common thought. How many people that have been considered wise have limited themselves to only thinking about their own well-being and their own desire(s) for a specific outcome? Answer: none.

Wisdom is about the removal of the Self from any equation while placing the greater understanding of the ever-expanding whole as the primary determinant. Wisdom is about focusing upon true reality not individualized reality.

Take a moment right now and define what you believe to be wisdom. Now, ask yourself, why do you believe what you believe to be wise is a quality of wisdom?

For each person we transverse through our life. For each person we inch our way through life as we find a means of survival. For each person we encounter life defined by the way we interact with others, what we do to others, and where we find ourselves in time and in culture, and mostly by what we think leading to what we do.

What do you think about? Do you follow a pathway guiding you towards developed wisdom or do you follow a pathway defined by all the whatever of undefined, unenlightened, human existence?

Those who walk towards wisdom, those who encounter wisdom, are those who remove themselves from the boundaries of individualized interpretation of thought and of action. They step beyond the realms of selfish Self and move their mind outwards towards a grander understanding.

Anyone can find wisdom. It is not as illusive as it sounds. Anyone can move towards a deeper understanding of life and of human consciousness. You just have to decide to try.

Embrace wisdom.

* * *

13/Jul/2020 01:01 PM

If you were to be judged for all of your bad deeds, even the ones you felt you were justified in doing, would you be going to heaven or would you be going to hell?

* * *

13/Jul/2020 01:00 PM

Who or what has guided you to think the way that you think?

You Want Something Done Right?
13/Jul/2020 10:34 AM

In all things life, there is one person who is the inception of that thing. There is one person who envisions it and then moves forward with its creation. From that point, yes, many a person may become involved but all things life can be traced back to one individual.

One individual is the sourcepoint. Sometimes the idea ends with them. They think it, they envision it, but they do not have the ability or the mentality to bring it into reality. In other cases, a person creates an idea and someone else runs away with it. They may do this by crediting their sourcepoint of inspiration or they may simply steal the idea outright. Whatever the case, there will forever be the creator and there will forever be those who aid or help in the extension of the concept.

Think about your own life. What part have you played in creation? What part have you played in the expansion of an idea created by someone else? Did what you did, help the growth and development of that idea or did it hurt its process of evolution?

Looking to your own involvement in the process of creation and/or the disbursement of an idea is an ideal method for you to come to an understanding about who and what you truly are.

Look to your life; what have you created? What idea did you come up with and what did you do to move that idea foreword? Look to your life; who's ideas have you helped to expand? And, why did you do either?

Many times in life, for an idea to move forward, the creator needs help. In some cases people willingly offer their services. I know in my life, people have come forward and helped me, particularly in the creation of films, and I was always so thankful for their help.

There is also a downside to this, however, a downside to a person's help that you may never see coming. In some cases, the people who offered to help me became lost in some hidden agenda or emotionally driven motivator and set about to completely hurt the process of cinematic creation. I never saw it coming so I could not prepare for it. Thus, their help became a hindrance and all that could have been lived and accomplished was lost.

On the other side of the issue, in my own life, I have always attempted to help people. Whether it was helping my martial art instructors by teaching their classes for them for free onto helping other filmmakers in whatever way I could. Those are simply a couple of examples but the key element to help is caring enough to take the time out of your life and your own mental melodrama to help. How much of that have you done?

So many people are locked into their own Mind Game. They only think about themselves. This is even the case when they are thinking about someone else. For example, there have been times when someone attacked my motives or credibility. I cannot tell you how many times, after the fact, that people have contacted me and said they were sorry about what happened to me. My response to them always was/is, *"Why didn't you do something about it?"* To which, they never have an answer. Thus, they did not participation in the creation or the implementation of anything. Like most, they simply sat back and watched.

I don't really care about the adolescent-minded nonsense unleashed by the unenlightened. But, I do appreciate the words of kindness. This being said, and it takes us back to the point in a person's involvement in the idea creation of someone else, I have also witnessed the damage that negative words and behavior can unleash on a concept, idea, or creation. Thus, it is important to understand that involvement in the ideas and creations of someone else takes on many forms.

But, this is the whole reality of life and this takes us to the source of inception. A person envisions and possible creates something; from there, people either dismiss it or latch onto it, and from this, in many cases, these outside entities/these people, create their life.

Maybe that initial idea was inspirational to a person, in either a positive or a negative manner. But, it was not their idea. That idea came from someone else, and from there, all kinds of life thoughts and life actions were created—created by the initial idea of someone else and then enacted upon by whomever.

There's the old saying, *"You want something done right, you've got to do it yourself."* But, you can't do everything yourself. You must include others. But, the moment others are involved, all kinds of individualized Mind Stuff is brought to the table. So, what's the answer? Well, the answer begins with you. It begins with what you create, what you do with your creation after it was created, who you allow to help you, and who steals your ideas as a reason to motivate their own actions. It's complicated, I know…

As we all understand, many people in their world are not good people. They steal other people's ideas and they use them to make money, to make a name for themselves, to gain notoriety, and to get whatever... Everywhere you look you see this. But, how many people actually think about this? Very few. They simply react to the reaction.

If you want something done right, you've got to do it yourself. If you allow other people to participate, you must be as careful as you can. But, the reality of reality is, most people are not creative people, they do not come up with their own ideas, thus, they steal the inspirations of someone else. So, you must simply be aware of that and never follow those who are not the sourcepoint of the inspiration, because individual inspiration is the foundation of all things creative, all things good in this world.

If you want to do the ultimate good, be the basis of your own creation. If you want to help, be the one who credits the creator and help them make their unique idea as grand as it can be.

* * *

12/Jul/2020 07:48 AM

Half full or half empty is based upon how much coffee you pour into your cup.

Controlling the Narrative
11/Jul/2020 08:07 AM

If someone asks you a question about yourself you can answer by telling them the truth or telling them a lie. Of course, we all understand, that telling the truth is the most honorable thing to do but, think about it, people lie all the time. Do you?

If someone asks someone else a question about you they can answer by telling them the truth or telling them a lie. Of course, we all understand, that telling the truth is the most honorable thing to do but, think about it, people lie all the time. How do you know that they are not lying?

The thing is, when someone else is speaking about you they have no vested interest. Sure, they may love you or they may hate you, they may want you to succeed or they may want you to fail, they may know you or they may only know of you, but whatever they say about you is only based upon their perception of you—they are not you so they cannot know the true you.

People surrender themselves to the narration of others all the time. Some do this because they hope to not have to discuss the truth of their life with someone face-to-face. Other do it because of the promised hope that someone else will make their life sound better than it actually is. Some do it simply because they are lazy.

The narration of a person's life is also commonly taken away from a person without asking. Think of all the people talking, discussing, and biography-ing the life of other people that they may or may not know. How about you? Who do you speak about and why? How do you describe that person? And, why are you saying what you are saying about them?

In the religious world, religious teachers speak of the grand entities all the time. They describe how they must have been feeling, what they must have been thinking, what they must have been doing, and why they were doing what they did. But, how do they know? This is only speculation, at best. Yet, think of all the books that have been written by people describing the life and the works of spiritual teachers. Think of all the books that have been written describing the life of the person who did something that someone finds noteworthy. Trillions and trillions of word have been spoken and written about that someone else—spoken and written by that person who was not them—maybe they had never even met them. Yet, the words are spoken, the words are written and decisions are made about an individual based upon those words. Doesn't this all seem a little convoluted and disingenuous?

Here's the reality, any word spoken or written by a person about another person can never be based in truth. At best, it is solely based in interpretation—elucidation about what somebody thinks about someone else.

Here's the reality, the only person you can actually listen to, with any hopes of understanding the truth of their life and their reality, is the person themselves, as they are the only sourcepoint of their reality. But, people lie. People alter the truth of their feelings, their emotions, and their life experiences to be accepted (or rejected) by those they are communing with. Think about it, how many times have you altered what you lived and what you felt when you were describing your life to someone so that they will find your experience(s) more palatable?

Thus, the truth of the truth is only in the Self. The truth of the truth can only be known by the Self. For it is only within the boundaries of your own body and your own mind that the truth of reality is the truth of reality—at least the truth of your reality.

If you look outside of yourself for a reason to have something to think about or to be emotionally motivated, all you have done is to lose sight of the truth of your own reality. If you are thinking or speaking about that someone else, you have removed yourself from a place where truth can actually be experienced.

If you broadcast your reality to others, at best all you have done is to create a fairy tale of how you wish your life to be projected. Thus, you are not telling the truth, you are only describing a depiction of how you want your truth to be perceived.

If you want to live a refined life, based in truth, stop trying to control the narrative and step into the place of inner truth, which is inside all of us. There, you will experience a place where you will encounter no need to embrace a false reality, where you are thinking and speaking about all of those things that are not based in the absolute truth of the Inner Self. This place where the lack of false, projected, reality exists is the only place where true Inner Truth may be experienced. This is the only place where you can come to a true sense of Self-Awareness.

Seeking Enlightenment
09/Jul/2020 08:05 AM

So, what are you planning to do today? What are your plans for your life and for you?

What do you do everyday? What do you think about doing? What do you desire?

Is your life motivated by you making money, making friends, finding lovers, being respected, being loved, being liked, climbing the ladder of life, or getting new possession? Are you driven to making your body the best it can be or to excelling at your job? Why is what you think what you think about? Do you ever contemplate finding enlightenment?

I get it, few people ponder moving towards cosmic understanding. But, why is that? I suppose there are many reasons but mostly it is not a concept that is integrated into our mindset, at least not here in the West. But, if you follow the path of your thoughts, (what you commonly think about), that have lead to you living your life the way you have, it is almost certain that you have encountered a fair share of turmoil; everybody has.

Here's the thing… There is another reality out there where your mind is not bound by your desires and the desires of others leading to conflict. It is a place/a space of freedom. It is a space of calmed understanding where as all things are as they are, they are.

The concept of enlightenment has been spoken about since the dawning of advancing human consciousness. It has always been placed out there in the far off distance, obtainable only by the most holy few. I won't go into the deliberation of that is why so few obtain enlightenment—even those who try, because by its very concept it is so hard to achieve. What I will say is that a clear and enlightened state of mind is extremely obtainable if only you decide to take your focus off of the You that is perceived by the world, the You who wants this and that, the You who thinks you are right and they are wrong, and all that kind of Mind Stuff, and simply let go and exist in a state of grace. It is doable. In fact, it is easily doable. You simply have to let go.

Here's your assignment for the day; let go. Right now, STOP, let your mind fall silence and let go. Let go of all that Mind Stuff that is reverberating around in your mind: all your likes, all your dislikes, all your agreements, all your disagreements, and all your desires of what you want and the way you want things to be.

What's on your mind? Let go of that right now and simply embrace the freedom of No Thought. If you do this, if you did this, you immediately felt it and you had your first glimpse of Satori. You felt what enlightenment is. Mind freedom.

Do this now. Do this today. Do this every time you have a chance. Do this every time turmoil comes your direction. Do this and you will come to know that there is place of illuminated freedom where you do not have to be bound by your desires, the desires of others, and the constrains of the world. Do this, and you too will understand enlightenment.

*   *   *

08/Jul/2020 08:48 AM

How many mistakes have you made?

The People That Keep You From Becoming
08/Jul/2020 07:37 AM

I was watching this movie, Wasp Network, the other night. Basically it's a character driven movie focusing on the interaction of Cuban and U.S. politics. As it's focus is Cuba, and the people from Cuba, they showed a clip of Fidel Castro. It sent me to remembering…

When I was in grad school at Cal State, L.A., my advisor was this one man—names shall remain nameless. In any case, my girlfriend at that time was a close relative to Fidel Castro. It was my idea, due to the fact that I had access to him, is that I would travel to Cuba with her, (which wasn't easy for U.S. citizens back then), and base my thesis around some aspect of his life, the revolution, and his administration. I thought it would be revolutionary to write that thesis. My advisor was totally against it, however. In fact, he refused to let me write a thesis on that subject. Why? I never really knew. Jealousy? Maybe. But, by his refusal he really screw up my thesis process, ultimately messing with the evolution of my life.

People mess with the life of other people all the time. Sometimes, as in the case with my graduate advisor, it is very direct. It is based in something that is only in their mind. They cast their judgment. They proclaim their declaration. And, that is that. What they do really damaged the life of the someone else. Do they care? I don't know. I guess each case is different. But, they did it because they could do it. In some cases, their action is very direct. In other cases, it is very indirect. But, in the end, all that is left was what was done that hurt the life evolution of someone.

Take a moment right now and think back through your life… Was there a time; was there a person who did something very specific that kept you from becoming? Who was that person to you? How did what they did affect your life then? How is it affecting it now? What part did you play in the evolution of that event?

Now, turn this around… Think back through your life, is there someone who you stopped from becoming? Is there someone where you did something that kept them from doing what they wanted to do? Is there someone where you did something that kept them from achieving from what they hoped to achieve? Why did you do that? Who would they have become in their life if you had not stopped them from becoming? Who are they now compared to what they could have become if you had not gotten in their way? How do you feel about that? Do you care? Do you ever think about them instead of only thinking about you?

Life is lived via personal interactions. Some of these interactions are small; others are much larger. The thing is, sometimes these interactions get in the way of us becoming. And, in some cases, there is nothing we can do about it.

I can say that you should be caring and understanding enough to never do anything to inhibit the growth and progression of anyone but will you listen? Virtually everybody who does something has a reason for doing it. Many times, it is simply their own reason that is understood by no one else. But, that reason has the potential to change someone else's life.

The answer? I guess there is none. Life equals interactions. Advancement equals receiving the approval of someone else. So, we are all dammed to this same equation. The sad fact is, sometimes people get in our way and stop us from becoming who we hoped to become. Don't be that person.

Let me end here with an interesting side note. A few years later, I met this very accomplished girl who was really into me. What was curious was that she was the exact same relationship to Fulgencio Batista, (the president of the government that Castro overthrew), as my aforementioned girlfriend was to Fidel. But, it was a very crazy, indulgent time in my life and I was just not in the space for what she wanted, which was probably sad because she was a very nice girl. Did I keep her from becoming? Becoming mine. I don't know? Maybe. Sometimes life is very complicated…

The Basis of Judgment
07/Jul/2020 02:22 PM

"For with what judgment ye judge, ye shall be judged: and with what measure ye mete, it shall be measured to you again." Matthew 7:2

I am forever intrigued by the way people judge people and how they dish out their condemnations onto others. I am forever fascinated how people listen to what other people say, believe without personal investigation, and then conclude that whatever that someone else said must be the truth simply because they said it.

I am also forever captivated in the way people react when they are harshly judged, even though, one upon a time, they were the one casting the judgment. *"Why is this happening to me,"* is the common question and, *"Who is that person to judge me,"* is the common follow up statement. Yet, judgment is all around us. Listen anywhere and you will hear it, look anywhere and you can read it. But, what is the basis of any of it?

The basis of judgment is a person's bias. What feds a person's bias? Who knows, it could be any number of things? The one thing that is for sure is that it is based upon a lack of understanding of the person they are judging. It is they deciding that the person they are judging is wrong based upon their own personal perception of reality. Their reality not true reality. It is they decided that they do not like what another person has done. But, that is just what they are thinking. It is simply what they believe. Is what another person believes about someone else the truth? Or, is it simply what they think about what they are thinking about?

View your own life. Think about the people you have judged. Pull a memory from your mind and analyze why you judged or criticized another human being. What was your motivation? Why did you do it? When you were doing it, were you even considering why you were doing it? Or, was it simply you believing your had a better understanding of who someone else was or why someone else was doing what they were doing then they did themselves?

Most people never contemplate why they judge a person or the things a person does. This is where all the problems from judgment arise. People just unleash their judgments without forethought. If they have forethought, if they do possess a plan in what they are doing, then what that plan is almost always universally based upon is the desire to cause someone else damage. But, how is damage ever a good thing? How is it ever a righteous thing? How and why does anyone ever have that right?

Matthew 7:2 provides us with an ideal example of what will happen to the judgmental person. But, who ever pays attention to the wisdom presented in books like the bible? People just react. As Descartes stated, *"I think I am therefore I am."* Most people operate from a sense of self-initialed, self-worth. They believe they have the right to say whatever it is they feel like saying no matter the consequences to the life of anyone else. They feel they have the right until it is done to them and then they question how that critical person possess the right to cast a judgment onto their life.

The conscious person knows how to live consciously. The good person knows how to live a life based upon goodness. But, how many of those people are out there? Are you one of them? Are you a conscious and good person? Or, are you a person who feels that your opinion about someone or something else should be heard, setting chaos in the life of that person or that thing into motion?

If you based your life upon unleashing judgment, judgment will find you. Don't you think it's simply a better option to allow people to be who they are, create what they create, and not assign your approval or disapproval onto it?

"For with what judgment ye judge, ye shall be judged: and with what measure ye mete, it shall be measured to you again."

* * *
06/Jul/2020 09:18 AM

In the realm of relationships; when you replace someone with somebody else, if you haven't changed what has changed?

Re-Meeting Our Past
05/Jul/2020 09:06 AM

In each of our lives there are people that we liked, people that we didn't like, people that we loved, people that we hated, people that became our friends, people that became our lovers, people we respected, people we learned from, people who learned from us, and people who stole from us. The relationships that people encounter in life run the gamut from good to bad and everywhere in between.

In most cases, people do not stay in our life forever. Most relationships move along and they are lost to the hands of the time. But, where did those people go? What became of them? What do they look like now? What became of their life? What did they do and what are they doing? It is inevitable that as we pass through the time(s) of our life the memory of these past relationships will come to mind and we will occasionally think of those people who passed through our life.

Though the world has changed vastly in the past few decades and it is much easier to find a person of your past, if that is what you really want to do, most people do not do this, however, because that's all a little creepy. This being said, I doubt that there is anyone who has not typed an old friend or an old lovers name into Google just to see what pops up. Most of the time nothing comes up, so that quest is put aside and one moves on with their life, as the memory of that person once again fades away. Sometimes, something does show up, however: a link, a social media account, a website, a photo and then many of the questions are answered.

But, all of that/any of that does not really provide a true picture into the life of any person.

This story comes to mind that was told on NPR one day as I was driving. A lady was describing how people project a certain image to the world, especially via the internet. She lived in a house where if you took a photo of it from one side the house and the neighborhood looked very nice. So, this is where she always focused her home-based social media photographs. But, she lived right next-door to a factory. So, if anyone were to see where she actually lived they may be appalled.

This is kind of like life. People want to put their best foot forward. They want to look as good as they can. They want to be perceived as something good. To achieve this people do all kinds of things, from using photo apps, to embellishing, onto straight out lying. But, do any of those things change who a person truly is? Only if you know them do you know but you no longer know them, so what is the truth?

Take a moment, think about someone from your past that you occasionally think about. Maybe take a another moment and seek them out on the internet. What did you find out? Did you find out anything? If you did find something, did they become what you thought they would become? Do they look like you thought they would look?

Most people chart out a life for themselves as they pass through their existence. They are living what they are living and they do not want their past to come back to haunt them. Most people understand that. They understand that because they are living their own life.

Some people never developed what may be considered a true life, however. They never got married, had a family, had a career, and did all of those things that most people do. From this, this style of person is often locked into remembering the past that is only in their mind and find it difficult to live in their now as their now is not fulfilling.

Though our past defines all of us and is even, in some cases, fun to remember. The past is not the now. Though many people view their past in terms of this now, they are deluding themselves.

So what does all of this tell us? It tells us that we are each all the same. We live our now (as best as we can) but we still remember our past. Though our past is what formed us to be what we are now, the past is not our now, and even if you may reconnect with that person from your past, you and they have lived a million experiences since then that the other person may never truly understand.

The fact is, all any of us can/should do is to love our now as best as we can. We do what we do and hopefully live a fulfilled life while hurting no one and helping many. Hopefully we can care, give, love, and nourish so anybody who remembers us will think of us fondly.

Your past is only your past. Even though other people may have taken part in it, you were the only one truly experiencing what you were experiencing. Think about that when you think about someone from your past. You are not they, just as they are not you. Their life became their life just as your life became yours. We all remember our past but what is more important is to truly live your now and make your now something worth remembering.

Helping Without Seeking Reward
03/Jul/2020 07:33 AM

A couple of months ago, during the height of the Coronavirus COVID-19 Pandemic Lock Down, I was taking an afternoon walk. It was kinda crazy that in a city like L.A. there were virtually no cars on the road.

I was walking down one of those streets with no sidewalk when I noticed this baby snake trying to get up the curb but he (or she) was too small and couldn't do it. The snake had probably come down to bask in the sun and wanted to get back home. Seeing this, I picked the snake up and put it back in the bush. No big deal. But, I was glad that I did as a few minutes later one of those big street clearing trucks came down the road and if the snake was still there it probably would have gotten killed.

It was easy for me to help the snake out. I saved its life. Did the snake even know what I had done for him? Most probably not. And, that's okay.

This is the thing about helping. It can be such a small, easy thing but it can save someone's life. Helping is really a good thing.

Most people only help someone when they know they are going to be thanked or paid in some manner at the end of the help. They want acknowledgement for their helping. They do what they do based upon the acknowledgement they plan to receive. But, is that really helping or is that just doing business?

Care enough to help someone. Turn off all of that need to be thanks or paid. Just help someone/anyone whenever you can. If you see they need help, help them.

Help people you know. Help people you don't know. Help people you love. Help people you hate. Help people you will never see again. Help and don't do it for the reward, do it because you can.

Helping is really one of the highest goods.

The Things That Nobody Knows
02/Jul/2020 03:45 PM

For each of us there are things in our lives that only we know. There are experiences and feelings that only we felt. Though other people may have been involved, it was only us who experienced them and integrated them into our life in our own, unique, and specific manner.

Think about something in your life that you experienced. This may be something very big or it may be something very small. But, what defines it is that it was only you who lived through it and only you who, at least initially, knew about it happening.

Maybe this was some physical event that happened to you. Maybe it was some physical event that you chose to take part in. Maybe it was some physical or mental event that you were forced to take part in. Maybe it was something that you witnessed that caused you to feel a certain type of way. Whatever the case, it was only you, there in that moment, living what you were living and feeling what you were feeling.

Have you ever wanted someone else to know about that experience or that feeling? Have you ever wanted to tell it to some specific somebody or scream it to the entire world? Have you ever wanted someone else to know about it but due to the various circumstances of your life, you could not/you did not tell anyone? Why not? Have you ever taken the time to define that why not?

In some cases, when you are close to someone, you have the ability to tell them pretty much anything be it good, great, horrendous, or meaningless. In other cases, however, sometimes telling a person or the entire world your story seems near impossible.

Certainly, in our currently place in time and history, spreading your feelings to the world is much more easy. It is easy, if that is what you really want to do. But, the problem with social media is that it has the tendency to backfire on people with all those adolescent minded judgmental people out there casting harsh judgments—judgments that they have no right to unleash. So, even though we live in a time where you can transmit your experiences more easily, the price you pay may be too high so, again, in some cases, you choose to keep things to yourself.

Take a moment right now and isolate one of those life events. One of those events in your past that you lived through and you wanted to tell someone (maybe one specific person) but you did not or you could not because you knew that if they knew about the occurrence it would change the way that they felt about you. Isolate that one event. Know what you were feeling and why you were feeling it.

Now, move past that event. Travel to that place where you wanted that specific someone to know about it but you could not tell him or her. Study your feelings of why. Know why you did not tell them. Think about that choice now, in retrospect, was it the right choice to make? How has your life evolved with them not knowing? How has your relationship evolved? Are you glad you did not tell them?

Turn this around now. Think about a very specific life event that you did tell someone about but you wish that you did not. Know the life event. Know your feelings about that life event. Know what you were feeling when you told that someone else about that life event. What were you hoping to gain from telling them? Study how they behaved and how they reacted. Why do you now wish that you had not told them? How has your life evolved with them knowing? How has your relationship evolved?

In life, we learn from experience. We learn from the experiences we experience and we learn by studying others and how they relate and react to our experiences.

It would be a great world if every one was caring, sympathetic, and understanding. Sadly, many people are not like that. Even people we think we know sometimes surprise us and show their true colors when we relay to them something that they find offensive.

Everybody feels what everybody feels. Each person processes their feelings in their own unique manner. Each person translates the experiences and the feelings relayed to them by other people in their own unique manner. Some are caring, thoughtful, and accepting. Some are harsh and judgmental. But, the reality of life is, if we do not express our life experiences to anyone then our life was lived in silence. Though this sounds very Zen, if this is the case, no one can truly understand who we are and why we are who we have become.

It's a hard choice sometimes to know whom you should tell what to. It can change the dynamic of the relationship. It can change the trajectory of the relationship. But, if a person who you are close to does not know the true you and what you have experienced to become the true you, what is your relationship built upon? Moreover, if the person you relay that something to turns out to be a un-

understanding jerk, isn't it better that you know the truth about who they truly are?

If you watch how people judge other people, you will know how they will judge you.

Looking for Inspiration
01/Jul/2020 12:26 PM

For those of us who consider ourselves artist, we are constantly seeking inspiration. So often people contact me and ask, where can they find their inspiration when they feel their creative well has run dry? For me, I'm just overwhelmed with it—there's so many things I want to create. But, more than that, I don't fight to find inspiration. If it's there, it's there. If it's not, it's not. And, I believe that's the problem many artists encounter. They try to force their inspiration. They try to force themselves to do. But, if you force anything, it's not natural and from this all of the spontaneity of the art (whatever that art may be) is either lost or severally inhibited.

This being said, and to answer the question, inspiration is really everywhere. You just have to be open up to it. Look around you. Listen. Watch the news. Go to the museum. Go to the supermarket. Take a walk. If you open yourself up to it, if you can understand that inspiration is not some defined something, then it can come to you from anywhere/everywhere.

For me, some of the people who have told me I was an inspiration to them, are the ones who are inspirational to me. What they do is great! It is unique. It is different. It is art. And, from there, I am inspired to explore new levels of doing.

Some people get locked into a very defined mindset—that their art and their inspiration must come from here and equal that. With this, the exploration of the new, the expansion of the different is forever lost. Art is forever new. Art is forever doing the different—even if that different is simply in the way you create your own art.

So, for those of you who seek inspiration, just open your eyes, listen, free your mind, and become the essence of art. Inspiration is everywhere.

Create!

* * *

30/Jun/2020 04:26 PM

Some people believe they are telling the truth but they are actually lying.

The Transmission of Information
30/Jun/2020 02:27 PM

  For anyone who knows about my martial art career, you know I have written a lot of articles for a lot of magazines in regard to the martial arts. I haven't really been doing that much lately and sometimes I receive questions about, *"Why not?"* The simple answer is, all the magazines went away. There are virtually no, in-print, martial art magazines left. The few that are still printed come out infrequently and don't pay their writers any money for the articles. And, the fact is, with photos and all that; it not only costs time but money to prepare those articles.

  In decades gone past, I have discussed how I was always so impressed when some of the articles in the martial art magazines were photographed by serious professionals. The techniques looked perfect. And, that was back in the days of film when you couldn't really see what the photograph you had taken looked like until it was developed. But, all that cost way too much money for a guy like me. So, I had to live with what I could get. A lot of times I hated the photographs and didn't really feel they displayed my ability or truly captured the technique. But, that's life when you are doing something/anything, sometimes you just have to accept the results and live with 'em.

  The thing that was great, or at least honorable, about that era in publication is that anybody couldn't get up on the pulpit and preach. There was checked and balances in place. There were editors between the writers and the readers. Things were fact checked. Copyrights were enforced. There was a system of right-ness.

So much has been lost since that era. Now, look on the internet, anybody says anything and people, simply because it is said, believe it.

Before, with the physical publications, their business structure and their editors enforced a formula. Sure, not everybody liked everything—there was a lot of criticism but you could at least believe what was presented. This was the same with books published by actual publishing companies. Not the plethora of self-published, self-motivated, un-fact checked writings that have recently flooded the world.

Now, I am not just some old guy pining for a long lost era. But, there is a lot that has been lost in the sources of where people gain their information. Anybody can say anything and they will find people to believe them. Is that the way life should be?

I was recently watching that documentary about the Amazing Randi. He is a magician who has spent much of his life debunking the way charlatans, so-called psychics, preachers, and the like get away with gaming the public and lining their pockets by performing slight of hand, by various means and methods. Think how much bullshit is out there. Bullshit spoken and written by people who are only playing on the unfulfilled needs of others in order to get paid. Though there has always been the con going on. But, with no checks and balances, with no need for elements of proof, something is really lost in the education and the transmission of information from mind to mind.

I come back to this point a lot in life. I sincerely feel people really need to investigate who is saying what and why. What is their motivation?

And, perhaps more importantly, what is your motivation for listening to what they have to say?

If you don't take the time to truly study the person who is speaking and ascertain their credentials and foundational wisdom for what they speak—if you don't take the time to know yourself to the degree that you know why you are listening to what anyone has to say, it is really easy for your life to be lead astray by someone who does not possess the qualifications to be teaching you (or anyone else) anything.

Not to belabor this point but I have met some really bad people who were willing to say and/or do whatever it took to get people separated from their money or to get them to consent to physical or mental submission. You've probably known a few of those people too.

As there is no more a system of checks and balances in the greater whole of the world, all this goes to looking before you leap, researching before you believe. It goes to knowing why you are getting your facts from whom you are getting them from. And mostly, it goes to you understanding you to the degree that you know why you are listening to anyone anyway.

Internet Bioville
30/Jun/2020 01:20 PM

I was sent this bio about me that somebody discovered on some ancient website. I always fin this kind of stuff very amusing. ☺

PS: The typos are not mine. This is just the way the bio was found.

Dr. Scott Shaw is one of the most advanced American practitioners of the art of Hapkido. He has a 8th-degree black belt in the art. He also holds an 8th-degree blackbelt in Tae Kwon Do, along with a 7th-degree black belt in Kumdo (Korean art of the Sword) and another 7th-degree black belt in Aikijutsu. In 1985, Scott went to Hong Kong to make his film debut in Blade in Hong Kong. From there, Scott knew that besides concentrating on the evolution of Hapkido, he also wanted to make some great entertaining action films. His work in Hong Kong would be the major influence for Dr. Shaw as he began to write, direct, and star in his own films. He has gained a great following with films like Samurai Vampire Bikers from Hell, and Legend of the Rollerblade 7. Scott will be best for 3 of his characters, tough as nails Alexander Hell, Rollerblade 7 leader Hawk, and Space Sheriff Jack B. Quick. Shaw uses a combination of his trademark martial arts skills and some various genres to make successful straight-to-video films. He even is a successful stunt co-ordinator, working on Toad Warrior: Hell Comes to Frogtown 3 in 1996. Shaw continues success as a prolific filmmaker as well as keeping up with the theories of Hapkido.

* * *
29/Jun/2020 05:25 PM

If you don't clean your space, wherever or whatever your space may be, it will remain forever dirty.

Emotional Verse Intellectual Understanding
29/Jun/2020 09:43 AM

Think about your life. Think about the things that you feel. Think about the way you feel about the things that you care about. Think about the way that you feel about the things outside of yourself. Think about the way that you feel about the things that you have no control over. Why do you feel the way you feel? Do you ever contemplate that?

Most people operate from a purely emotional perspective. Some people are very overtly emotional. They do not have a strong sense of control over the emotions. Other people know how to keep their emotions in check. They feel them, they operate from an emotional perspective, but they do not broadcast their emotions out to the world.

For the people who operate from an emotional perspective, whether they do this via an overt or subdued perspective, they define their life based upon the way they are feeling about whatever it is they are thinking about. They make their decision based upon what they are feeling. How about you? How is your life defined?

Emotional understanding is based upon a foundationless reality. Emotional understanding is formulated simply by the way a person feels. But, why does a person feel the way that they feel? How many people ever following their feelings to their sourcepoint and truly examine why they feel what they feel? Do you?

Most people do not. They simply feel what they feel but they never truly explore why they feel that way. As they do not truly know why they are feeling what they are feeling, these undefined emotions cause them to act out based upon an undefined conglomerate of information dominating their brain.

Some people operate from an intellectual perspective. They analyze all aspects of what they are encountering based upon a criteria of pure analytical investigation. From there, they make a choice on how to behave, how to act and react towards others, what decisions to make, and what to do based upon the facts that are available and presented to them.

Then, there are the people who play the Mind Game of seeking out facts to solidify their emotions. But, that is a completely different discussion.

How do you make decisions in your life? How do you decide what you are going to do? Is what you are going to do based upon factual evidence or are you motivated to action simply by emotion?

The difference between these two characterizations of understanding is that a life based upon emotion leads to emotional actions and reactions. ...You feeling the way you feel and then acting upon those emotions causing your life to be lived formulated by your emotions. The problem with living your life in this manner is that it also causes other people to have emotional reactions directed towards you.

It is not that living your life based solely upon emotion is bad or good; it is simply the fact that most people never contemplate about this defining element of their life. They simply feel, which causes them to act, which causes other people to react, which causes all of the emotion-based life events that take place all around us.

For the person who operates from an intellectual life perspective, though their choices are not always perfect or right, what they base their existence upon is a more refined state of consciousness leading to a life where what they say, what they do, and even what they feel can be backed up by rational and logical explanations.

Think about your own life. What has caused you to make the decision you have made, leading to what you have done? You may not have thought about those emotion-based things you did while you were doing them but take a moment right now, isolate a few specific cases in your life, and really trace your emotion-based actions to their source. Why did you do them?

Now, still viewing those isolated moments in your life, define how you would have handled that situation differently if you were operating from a perspective of factuality instead of simply emotion. What would you have done differently? How would your life have evolved differently? What would have been the impact on your life and what would have been the impact on the life of others?

Most people operate from the perspective of emotion. From this is born love, hate, admiration, and condemnation. But, emotion is not the concrete building block of progress: internally or externally. It is only emotion. It is only you feeling what you are feeling about whatever it is you are feeling it about. If you cannot separate yourself from your emotions your life and the life of all of those people you interact with will be caused to be defined simply by a random emotion you are feeling in a given moment of time. And, as we all realize, what you feel today may be very different from what you are feeling tomorrow.

Your life is your life. What you feel is what you feel. But, if you do not know the sourcepoint of your emotions, if you do not trace them to their source, all that occurs is that you will have existed in a life defined by the fleetingness of emotions that have not only impacted your existence but all of those your have encountered in your life.

If you do not know why you are feeling what you are feeling, you do not know you. If you do not know you, why should your emotions be allowed to influence and guide the life of anyone else?

If you don't know you facts, all you have is emotion. Emotions are as fleeting as the wind. Never let them come to be the defining factor of your life.

* * *
27/Jun/2020 03:28 PM

Just because you're saying something doesn't make it true.

Zen Consciousness and the Obliteration of Wasted Action
26/Jun/2020 09:48 AM

What is Zen Consciousness? Zen Consciousness if the way of encountering life with the understanding that all things are perfect—that all things are as they are and because they are what they are fighting with them only creates chaos leading to emotion creating actions that do not serve the purpose of the greater good.

Look at your life. Look at the things you have lived. Look at the good times in your life and look at the bad times in your life. What were all of those Life Things based upon? They were based upon your definition of those moments. Your characterization as to whether or not you liked what was happening or you did not like what was happening. But, do you ever question, where did those definitions of like or dislike arise?

If you look at any life situation you will most commonly find there are multiple elements in play. There is more than one person involved. In certain circumstances, most of the people involved will be feeling one certain way about what is taking place, be it a feeling of positivity or a sensation of negativity. But, there most commonly are a number of interpersonal definitions in play, as well.

If we break this idea down to two people; one person will be feeling one way, which is motivating their actions, while the other person will be feeling another way that is thereby causing them to experience and react. Even if two people feel fairly similarly about a specific life situation that is taking place, each of these people will hold their own subtle life interpretation of that moment. From this, we can come to understand that every life event is wholly defined in the mind of the individual. The more mentally refined the individual, the more they interpret each life event from a broader more cultivated understanding. Whereas the more emotional and unrefined individual will base everything, all of the actions and reactions, strictly upon their emotional response driven by whatever it is they like or dislike. But again, does an individual who bases their life upon emotionally based responses ever question, where did those definitions of like or dislike arise?

From the perspective of Zen Consciousness, one consciously removes these life obstacles from the equation by giving into the understanding that all life is perfect—that all things are as they are.

Think about it, if you operated from this perspective how simply and how free would your life become? You would not have experienced all the anger, frustration, hurt, and random emotions that have been the cornerstone of your life. Emotions that have led many people to do many bad things not only to the life of other people but to their own life evolution, as well.

The thing about Zen Consciousness is that it is so simple. It is so simply yet many argue their way away from it. They rationalize their feeling, they justify their actions, and they make excuses for their emotions. But, all any of this does is to lock the individual into the mindset of a life defined by turmoil.

Think about it, if you could just experience life as it is lived, if you can simply encounter each life experience without placing a definition upon it, how simple, how perfect would your life become?

If you wish to live a better life—if you hope to be freed from undefined emotions that lead you down the road to poor decisions, embrace Zen Consciousness.

* * *
24/Jun/2020 12:28 PM

How do you feel when you say something negative about a person?

How do you feel when someone says something negative about you?

Karuṇā
23/Jun/2020 08:27 AM

The Sanskrit word, *"Karuṇā,"* is translated as, *"Compassion."* Compassion is at the heart of a person walking the spiritual path, as compassion is the conscious motivator for a person to step beyond the boundaries of Self and reach out and care more about the other person than simply the self-serving mindset of caring about themselves.

Compassion is a complicated concept, however. For within its definition is how one interprets it, and from this, it is very common, that much of its true understanding is lost. For many, compassion is motivated simply by one person feeling sorry for another individual. But, the true understanding of compassion is much deeper than that. Compassion is as much about one person turning off their own desires in order to truly understand the life condition of someone else than it is simply about one person feeling sorry for someone else.

Think about your life; think about the people you have felt sorry for. Who are those people and why did you feel that emotion towards them? For most, that emotion arises when you see a person being hurt or damaged by the words or actions of someone else. Though this is a natural reaction in life, for those people who care enough to care about anyone but themselves, if you think about it, if that is the motivation for feeling compassion than it is more based upon superiority than benevolence. It is based upon the concept of they are living that lessor lifestyle or they are having that done to them and I am not. Let me help them.

In essence, that style of behavior, though giving, is based in ego, *"I can give this to you,"* rather than it being based in true compassion.

This is where compassion gets a little bit complicated and why the true Buddhist understating of compassion is rarely put into practice. True compassion is enacted by removing yourself from the equation and giving/helping from a space of refined consciousness where the thought of you or the idea of you giving is not involved. In other words, it is not actualized with the thought, *"I am doing this for them,"* or *"I am helping them,"* it is done from a space of absolute oneness where your action are based in the sense of helping the greater all, not simply you doing this for them.

Most people operate from the very low level of human consciousness where they based everything that they do upon a mindset of, *"Me."* They think what they think, they do what they do, but all of that doing is based upon what they think, what they want, and what they hope to achieve whether it is for themselves or for someone else. Most actions, which may be considered compassionate, are enacted from this frame of mind, as well. Though good is always better than bad—though giving is always better than taking, many people miss the point when they do the things they do that are geared towards helping other people. They miss the point because they are only seeing themselves as the sourcepoint of the action—they are only seeing themselves as the someone who is doing the something.

True compassion is based upon your doing, whatever good action it is you are doing, motivated by the perspective of removing yourself, your doing, and your giving from the equation and doing what you do based in an true expression of enhancing the greater good. Thus, all desire for any expected outcome, on your part, is removed—all hope for any gratitude or receiving any praise or reward, on your part, is absent from the motivation for your actions. That is how you can identify a truly companioned act—there is no sense of one person doing one thing that befits them in an manner.

True compassion is about you removing you from the equation of giving and simply providing another individual or a greater entity with what they truly need, not with what you want them to have or what you think that they need. Compassion is you giving from the most spiritually pure, egoless, and caring place in your being. It is you providing when <u>you</u> are not involved.

*   *   *
22/Jun/2020 08:41 AM

How much better would your life be if you could erase all of your mistakes?

* * *

21/Jun/2020 11:06 AM

Just because you get away with a crime doesn't mean you didn't commit the crime.

Think Good Things. Say Good Things. Do Good Things.
21/Jun/2020 08:53 AM

Certainly, there is nothing new about the concept of thinking, saying, and doing good things. I suggest that people do this all the time as do so many others. But, how many people do? How many people take control over their rambling mind and decide to only think, say, and do good things? Do you?

If look at the world, at this point in history, there is so much conflict going on. Do people have a reason to be angry? If they do, they do, that is their personal choice. Are some people seeking a change? Yes, it seems so. But, how a person interacts with the world, what they do and how they set change in motion, is the defining factor about how they live their life. It seems that most of the people who are thinking, speaking, and acting to invoke this change are doing so from a very rage-driven, angry perspective. There is a lot of destruction taking place. Even many of the people who are not out there in the streets and are simply thinking and feeling from their home are basing what they think and do upon a very negative perspective.

Take a moment and think about your own life. Think about the things you have thought, leading to the words you have spoken and the actions you have taken. What was the motivation for you thinking what you thought, leading to what you said and did? What did you hope to achieve? But, more importantly, why did you think what you thought leading to what you said and did? Did your thought(s) arise from your mind originally or where they inspired and spurred on by what someone else thought? Do you ever take the time to trace your thought to their source?

As your thoughts are the basis for all that you ultimately say and do, where did the thoughts you were/are thinking come from? And, why did that thought cause you to do what you have said and done?

If we look to the outside world, even if we simply watch the news, we can see all the chaos currently being invoked. Sure, there is presently a lot of mob mentality going on. But, at the root of any mob mentality is one person thinking one thing and from this they gather others of like mind together. But, if the Like Mind is based in a hurtful mindset, what occurs? Damage. Damage to the life and the livelihood of other people, leading to ever-expanding negativity, anger, and damage.

At the root of most people's thought process is them only thinking about they think, what they want, and what they hope to achieve. How about you? Who and/or what do you think about? How about right now? What are you thinking about? How is what you are thinking going to cause you to act and to react today?

It is easy to take control over your thoughts and decide to think good/positive things leading to you performing good/positive actions. Most people simply do not choose to do it. They prefer to be invigorated by the mindset of attack. But, if any of these people would take the time to trace their thoughts back to their source they would find that their anger, their frustration, their judgment is arising from something outside of themselves—it is/it was cultivated by something someone else spoke or did to them. The fact of the fact is, most everything you are thinking and feeling was instigated in your mind by someone out there. This instigation may have been direct, by someone telling you something or it may be indirect, what someone said about you or did to you, but whatever the case, all of this leads to one conclusion; that conclusion is, you are allowing other people to control what you think leading to what you do. Though most people refuse to acknowledge this fact.

The remedy to all of this is to take the time to trace your thoughts, equally your words and your actions, to their source. Seek out where you were inspired to think what you were/what you are thinking. At this point, once you reach the centerpoint of your mind you can then choose to take control of thoughts and for those who wish to live a better, more whole and helpful life path, you can decide to think about life from a positive perspective, leading to you only saying and doing good/positive things.

Think good things. Say good things. Do good things. You want your life to be better—you want there to be positive change in the world, then use that as your mantra.

Dancing in the Pretense
About What You Didn't Do
20/Jun/2020 07:28 AM

There is a certain group of people who does not do. Maybe they want to do, maybe they wish they could do, maybe they have even tried to do, but at the end of the day they did not do. What are they left with? The knowledge that they did not do.

This causes some people to live in a state of denial. They make excuses, they lie, they bob and they weave around the truth but at the end of each day what is the reality is the reality and the truth is, they did not accomplish anything. From this, many aberrant behaviors are given birth to. Most notably these people judge and/or criticize those people who have done. For these un-doers this is like a drug. It makes them feel like they are doing something, it makes them feel like they are contributing, it makes them feel like they are actually doing something but as they, themselves, have never done what they think and what they say holds no truth in the reality of suchness and accomplishment.

Have you ever asked a person for help and they could not give it to you? Have you ever asked a person for help and they did not give it to? What was their reason for not stepping up to the plate and providing you the help you asked for?

Everybody has a reason. Everybody has a self-generated mental motivation for doing what they do—this included their non-doing.

Some, you will find, will provide you with a very logical reasoning for why they did not help. Others, simply live in denial and they come up with all kinds of excuses. This style of dismissive behavior is particularly frustration when what you are asking an individual to do is based upon something that they have previous done to you that negatively altered the course of your life or upon the fact that you have done something for them and they owe you. But, no matter what their logical, if their response is their not doing, it is only you who is left with that unpaid debt from that individual, and, it is only you, not receiving the help or the doing that you need.

If you look to the life of people who have accomplished something with their life, universally their achievement is based upon their doing. But, the fact of life is, not everyone can be a doer. For any untold number of reasons some people cannot and will not do. Though you can fight tooth and nail with them, telling that they should do, but your words will fall to deaf ears. Yet, as is often the case, this person's un-doing may be more detrimental to their own life and to your life than anything that they could do if they would bring themselves to the doing.

So, where does this leave us in life? The answer, there are the people who do, there are the people who try to do, and there are the people who do not do. And, no matter how hard you try to make a non-doer do, it can and never will happen.

In life, not everyone will achieve what they want. That's simply a fact of life. In life, not everyone will own all that they want. That's just reality. But, if you don't try then you will not have tried. If you do not do, you cannot achieve. But, if some non-doer will not help you do, do not allow yourself to have your life defined by their not-doing. Do not allow your life to be defined by their lack of achievement. For just as all you are is all you are, all they are is all they are. If they cannot do that should never stop you from your ongoing doing. For, doing is the sourcepoint of all achievement and without achievement nothing changes.

* * *
20/Jun/2020 07:27 AM

There is no justification and there is no excuse for hurting the life of anybody for any reason.

* * *

19/Jun/2020 08:10 AM

Some people attempt to make others believe that their options actually matter by screaming their opinions as loudly a possible.

*   *   *
17/Jun/2020 02:39 PM

What have you done today to hurt the life of somebody you don't know?

What have you done today to help the life of somebody you don't know?

The Roller Blade Seven: Let's Talk About the Edit
16/Jun/2020 04:53 PM

I remember reading a review written about *The Roller Blade Seven* a long time ago and the reviewer said something to the effect, *"I think they really wanted to make Easy Rider."* Of all the reviews I have read about the film, both positive and negative, that sentence was the closest to understanding what we were doing than anything else that had or has been spoken or written about RB7.

There has been so much talk about this film since its release and as I have said far too many times, *"There is rarely a week that goes by when someone does not ask me something about that film."* And, that's fine! I'm glad that people are still discovering it—seeking it out and trying to figure it out.

Some of what I am going to say in this piece I have said before. Other things will be more unknown. But, it is essential to understand that at the heart of *The Roller Blade Seven* is art. That was where both Donald G. Jackson and myself were coming from when we made the film. Don and I were/are both artists. Everything we did in association with that film was done so from a position of cinematic art.

Imagine begin able to make a movie exactly as you would like to. Imagine having CCC, Complete Creative Control. That was how RB7 was made. Though we had a few problems introduced to us by our Executive Producer, no one told us what to do, how to do it, or what we could or could not do. We did exactly what we wanted to do. This also goes to the editing of this film. We created cinematic art based upon what we had available to us at the time.

So, let's get to the edit…

As has been well documented, I was the editor of *Roller Blade Seven*.

As a note; as I write this piece I am also discussing *Return of the Roller Blade Seven*. But, to keep it simple, I will simply be stating *Roller Blade Seven* when discussing these two Zen Films.

Roller Blade Seven was the first time I had ever edited a movie. We initially took the movie to an editor Don had worked with in the past. A nice guy, but he just was far too mainstream for what we were trying to achieve. His mistake, if you want to call it that, was that he showed me how to use the editing equipment. From this, I went off into a separate editing bay and I put together a couple of scenes. Don saw them and was blown away. *"That's what I want,"* he exclaimed. The original editor, after seeing my edits, realized his mistake in teaching me how to use the equipment. All he could say was, *"I may have trimmed a few frames a little bit off of the end of one of those clips."*

In terms of Don, he had the strangest reaction. I could just feel it—feel it bleeding onto me; it was like he became so proud. He was so proud of me, so proud of our connection, so proud of my edit. Though these words really do not do the emotion justice, this is the closest I can come to explaining it. He just radiated.

Soon after this, post the original editor telling Don that we were trying to, *"Push the envelope too far,"* he was gone. Don and I relocated to a new editing suit over at the Beverly Connection in West Hollywood and aside from the actress induced drug and sex filled debauchery that took place in that editing suite, I sat there editing the film.

As one of Don's short-term friends, who he quickly ended up hating, exclaimed when he came by our editing suite, *"Does this kind of stuff really go on?"* My response, *"Yes, it does."*

The edit for RB7 took place very organically. It grew and expanded as we begun to understand how we wanted to portray the film footage that we had created.

To step back a little bit, for anyone who understands the process of shooting a film on film, you will know that once a reel of film is shot, first it must be developed before any editing can take place. From there, at least in 1991, you would then take the film to a facility where Telecine would take place.

Telecine is a process where you correct or alter the color, sync the sound, and transfer the movie to time coded video tapes from where you can edit the film and then manually transfer the time code where the master of the film would be produced from the individual one-inch masters. As you can imagine, all this takes a lot of time and money.

Some of my best memories of making *The Roller Blade Seven* occurred during the Telecine process. We would film several hours of film and then go to the Telecine facility. There we would view our dailies with this great colorist we hired. He was this very cool African-American guy who dressed to the nines every day with silk shirts, cool colored leather jackets, and patent leather shoes. He was really great at his job! Don and I were in love with the golden hour so we altered the color of all of the outdoors scenes to reflect this time of day as much as possible. *"More gold,"* we continually exclaimed.

Each time we were there we sent out for chili from nearby Chili John's restaurant. And, we watched as the bones of the film took shape. Good times!

Once we had completed principal photography and Telecine is when we focused on the edit. The fact is, RB7 is one of those films that we could have filmed forever as we continued to come up with new ideas. But, as the 1992 American Film Market was approaching, we were given a deadline, thus, we had to wrap it up and we began the edit.

The edit for the RB7 was done with straight cuts, as that was our only option. We didn't possess the postproduction budget to pay for the then, what were very-very expensive, things like cross dissolves and the like. But, this turned out to be a good thing in the long run as it allowed us to make the cuts and the transitions of the movie very precise.

I know there has been a lot of talk about the fact that we repeat elements of a scene several times during transitional moments. There may be three, four, or even five flashes at the end of a segment. Some people have wrongly suggested that we did this to emulate the flash cuts of the higher budget martial art films that were popular at the time, where you may see a kick or a punch impact an opponent multiple times from different angles. This is wrong. That was not at all what we were doing. …Back to the subject of Easy Rider… If you see that film you will notice that they used flash cut edits to transition some of the scenes. That was our inspiration. Not martial art films.

As I was editing and came to the end of composing a scene, after having laid in three or four flash cut, I would look to Don and ask, *"What do you think,"* in regard to the number of flash cuts. *"Maybe one or two more,"* he would smilingly say... This edit technique was one of the signatures of the film.

People have also wrongly discussed the fact that we used takes more than once in the movie because we did not film enough footage. Again, this was not the case. By the end of principal photography we had over twenty-four of usable footage. The reason we reused some of the footage, from some of the scenes, was all based upon the presentation of cinematic art.

Here, we go to our stepping beyond the expected and the normal in terms of RB7 editing. This also takes us into the mind of cinematic art in association with this film. We were not just doing this to do it. We were doing it to reference a state of consciousness—not simply a state of drug-induced consciousness, but a state of altered reality consciousness.

For anyone who has used hallucinogenic drugs (and I do not recommend it) but you will understand that at certain times you begin to see long trails of light following the movement of anything. As stated, we didn't have the budget to do anything like that, but we could emulate the occurrence that happens when reality is presented to you more than once while under the influence. It is like sometimes reality flashes at you more than once and you are forced to study unique aspects of each viewing of the same situation. Each time you experience it, though it is exactly the same, it is very different and new realizations are had. That was our inspiration and our motivation.

We pretty much lived in that editing suite for a couple of weeks. And, one of the very weird things that I realized that begin to happen to me was that as my mind was so focused on the edit of each scene, I began to view life in edits. It was a really weird experience; each conversation I would have with a person, each time I would turn my head, or look in my rearview mirror as I was driving, it was like I was cutting the film of my life. It was weird…

Though there were a lot of interesting, fun, and hedonistic experiences that took place in that editing suite, editing RB7 was not without it's problems. The problems were all instigated at the hands of Don.

The first notable one occurred nearing the end of the edit. At the time, though I was living with my main girlfriend, I was seeing a number of other girls, as well; exploring the possibilities of those relationships. One of which, who I had met through casting RB7, hung out, and though she was very beautiful, Don just noted how quiet she was when she was around us. All good… The negative situation that occurred was with this other girl I was going out with. I had met her while filming a commercial just prior to going up on RB7. I was a beach playing volleyball guy and she was one of the girls cheering me on. She was a very nice, very pretty girl. She came by the editing suite one day and Don just went after her. Now, first of all, he was a chubby, balding, middle-aged guy. This girl was a beautiful Asian girl who came to Hollywood via Hawaii. I don't know what he was thinking but he was playing hard. He was breaking all of the rules of the guy code. I mean, I never went after the girls he had on the line. But, for some reason, this girl just sat there all day as we edited and took Don's inappropriate innuendos. Several times, Don tried to throw his power around, I guess to impress the girl, but he and I both knew he couldn't do the edit, so I just ignored him, though the way he was behaving did really piss me off. He eventually went home and the girl and I hooked up in the editing suite. The problem was, I had been in the suite all that day, all that night, and I woke up in there the next day. By the time I went out to get some breakfast, I was a fucking zombie having had my eyes buried into the footage of the film and not encountered the daylight or any fresh air in well over twenty-four hours.

The next problem occurred nearing the end of the Off-Line edit. Don, as has been well described, had a very chaotic personality. Though he and I, for the most part, got on very well, one day he freaked. It was while we were editing the footage that eventually became the first Zen Documentary, Interview. This footage is where we did this semi-faux interview about RB7 on Hollywood Blvd. It's an interesting watch. I recommend it. Anyway, I think what happened is that Don always liked to be the center of attention. And, while watching the footage for the first time, he realized too many of the questions were being directed my direction. I don't know what he expected but at one point he completed freaked out and started screaming and ponding the wall with his hand. Then, we walked out of the suite. I continued to edit. He came back in maybe a half an hour later and his face had gone pale, *"I think I broke my hand, Scott."* Which, he had done.

In the end, we decided to only use a very brief segment of that footage at the end of RB7. Which, turned out to be a good thing, because, as stated, it later become the first *Zen Documentary*.

After I completed the Off-Line edit we took it to an On-Line facility. This is where we would soundtrack the films and put the edited scenes together.

As I've talked about in other essays and in books in the past, this is where I was asked to do the soundtracks for the two films at the last minute. I had to create two entire soundtracks all in one weekend... This, in the analog age, long before the era of computer composition. But, that's not the focus of this piece. So, let's stay on the edit.

The On-Line facility is where the construction of the films: *The Roller Blade Seven* and *Return of the Roller Blade Seven* took place. One of their people watched the edited Off-Line footage and wrote down all of the time code that was then transferred into their system where the one inch masters where then put up, one at a time, and taken down as necessary as the final version of the film was constructed onto a one inch master. As you can imagine, this took a lot of time and cost some big money. We were there for a little over a week.

In terms of what this place provided to the edit and final completion of the film(s)... It is there that we laid in the M&E, (music and the sound effects), this is where the titles were created and laid in, and the final master copies of the films were created. Overall, it all went along pretty well. The one thing that did occur, that really taught me a lot about the filmmaking process, is in the scene where Allison's character skates away from Don Stroud. In that scene we had laid in this echoing laughter that carried on throughout her departure. It was a really nice sound effect. The problem was, as we were watching the final pass of the final master, somehow the On-Line editor had not laid it in. He knew it was missing. He immediately turned and looked to Don and I. The problem was, though it was his mistake, it would have been a very big DO to have to go back into the film and re-lay it down. It would have cost a lot of money. So, Don let it slide. I don't believe that I would have made that same choice, as it really added to the film. But, that's the reality of filmmaking; sometimes you simply have to let things go and live with what you get.

On that day, as we were watching the final master cuts of the two films, I had a very deep realization that had been building throughout the edit process. That realization was, though when we started this film, several months before, I thought it was going to emerge as a straight-ahead action adventure flick, but what these two films came to be are very inside movies. For Don and I, who were the only two people who were there everyday of preproduction, production, and postproduction, we knew what we were creating and why we were creating it. Watching the final versions of these films, I confirmed my belief that most people would/could never understand what we were doing or why.

I have always believed RB7 is one of those movies that is a personal experience. That's what we were shooting for and I believe what we achieved. RB7 is a unique experience that can only be truly understood by the interpretation of the individual. For me, one of the two filmmakers of the film, I know we created art. For other people, however, unless they have an awareness for mind bending cinematic art, they probably never will understand what we were trying to do.

Of all the things that are discussed about *The Roller Blade Seven,* in both a positive and a negative manner, the edit of this film is at the top of the list. As is always the case, in all aspects of *The Roller Blade Seven,* there are so many more specific stories I could tell you about the editing of this film. But, I will save those for a book I may or may not someday write. For, as like the movie, you really would need to possess a certain kind of mindset and have a true desire to spend the time to read those stories in order to truly understand this film's creation. I know most people don't hold this conviction.

So, that's the story… At least the story, in brief, about the editing of *The Roller Blade Seven.* For all of you viewers/reviewers out there, I trust this will add some understanding for you about the creation of this film. But, for most of you who do not or cannot understand cinematic art, I imagine that this piece will provide you with little grist for the mill.

* * *
16/Jun/2020 07:17 AM

Who decides the dreams that you will dream?

Questioning Your Vanity Controlling Your Ego
14/Jun/2020 07:26 AM

For those who walk the spiritual path, particularly for those who walk the path of eastern spirituality, they are taught that one should never let their ego or their vanity take control over and guide their life. They are taught that one must continually view what they are doing, how they are doing it, and why, and then remove any self-motivated thoughts and actions.

As so many people are schooled in the process of self-advancement, self-worth, and getting whatever it is an individual wants, at whatever cost, some would question why should they even be concern with the controlling of their ego? Here we come to the study of life definition and what is the true essence of an individual's life.

Is your life simply about you looking good, feeling good, doing what you want, being in control, and anybody else in the world who doesn't help you gain whatever it is you want be damned? Or, is your life about focusing on your higher self and raising your consciousness in order to be the best instrument of providing help, goodness, and service to the all and the everyone?

The truth is, most people only care about themselves. I am sure if you look to the interactions you have experienced in your life, with other people, you can point to the people who only cared about themselves and what they wanted and they did not care what they did to you or anybody else. They only focused on themselves. We've all encountered people like that. In a few other instances, however, you probably will be able to point to people who you understood to be a truly good person, a truly helping person. How did that person become that individual? Was it via only thinking about themselves; what they wanted and how good they looked getting it? Or, was it by them putting their self-desire, their self-image in check in order to look outwards from themselves towards the betterment of all?

Take a look at yourself. Do you live your life via a position of ego? Do you flaunt your accomplishment, your power, your good looks, your possessions or do you keep yourself and your ego in check and ask the other person what they need before you think about what you want?

You can live yourself from a position of vanity and ego, many people do. But, the one truth about living your life from this vantage point is that it never lasts. For a person who lives their life from this perspective encounters the same things that everyone does: time, age, embarrassments, and someone who is bigger and better. But, to the person who does not live their life from a position of vanity and ego, encountering these inevitable life events does not come to be a, *"Hurt."* They are simply a reality that can be laughed off. But, to the person who bases their life on vanity and ego, even the most minor undesired life encounter, becomes a knife in their heart.

You can live your life based on your ego if you want to. That is your choice. But, if on the other hand, you choose to constantly be reflective enough to keep your ego in check, you cannot imagine the freedom of mind you will encounter. You cannot not imagine how much good you can do for the all and the everyone else.

The ultimate question you have to ask yourself is, are you the only one who matters? Or, does everyone matter? Is everyone, and how they feel, just as important as you?

You can focus on yourself and maybe you can look good and people will flock to you, if only for a moment. Or, you can care about the everybody else, and you can make the world just a little bit better place. Your choice.

Love Everything That Exists In This Moment and You Will Be Free
12/Jun/2020 01:28 PM

"Love everything that exists in this moment and you will be free." I am told that someone quoted a passage from one of my books on Twitter yesterday. I believe I wrote that passage for the book, *About Peace: 108 Ways to be at Peace When Things Are Out of Control.*

I stand by that statement. But, what about when you are not in love with everything in your moment?

From a spiritual and psychological perspective I can say that what you experience is truly defined by your mind. It is defined by how you choose to view the world, the world situation, and your situation. In other words, you make the choice on how you feel about anything that you are encountering. The problem is, most people never possess the mental fortitude to control their thoughts or their emotions so they simply react to what they are experiencing.

Even me, the man who wrote those words many-many years ago, when I remove myself from the space of mental control, I too feel what I feel about whatever situation I find myself living.

For example, I was in *Trader Joes* today buying some groceries. For those of you who may not know, *Trader Joes* is what I may deem a, *"New Age,"* supermarket. Originating in California, it's been around for a long time now and all of their locations are staffed by what I would term, off-beat (in a good way), friendly, smiley people.

As this COVID-19 pandemic has taken control over the world, everything has changed. In the past few days, this one location of *Trader Joes* has put whale stickers on the ground, a couple of feet back from the cash registers, where the cashiers are protected by Plexiglas. When you are directed to move forward towards the cashier, you are told to stand on the sticker until you are asked to pay. …Okay, that's what's going on with the world now. I get it. The virus is infecting and killing so many people. People need to be protected. Especially those people who provide essential services like working in supermarkets. But, I hate it! Everyone is hidden behind masks; you can never see the pretty smiling faces of people. And, the world is just a mess.

I keep coming back to the thought of why is no one super pissed off at China? They destroyed the world! I know, I know, everything is so Politically Correct now and you are not supposed to be saying things like this. And, this certainly has nothing to do with race. But, think about it, you take all the terrorist attacks and all the cyber attacks that have taken place over recent years and all those intentional actions have done far less damage than COVID-19 that originated in China.

China has destroyed the world! How many people have become sick? How many people have died? How much financial ruin has this pandemic caused? All because of China.

Now, for the record, China does not like me. I'll never be able to go back because they refuse to issue me a visa. That's probably a good thing because if I did return they would probably arrest me on some trumped up change and fuck my life over big time.

You know, I was one of the early people to travel to China when they were first opening up what was then called the Bamboo Curtin. I've had a lot of experience in China. ...Even a few encounters with the, (for lack of a better term), governmental secret police.

China is a beautiful place. Many of its people are beautiful beings. I wish I could go back. All that being said, from the moment I first traveled to China I knew they would ultimately emerge as the world's most super Super Power. Why? Because they had/have an endless supply of people that are scared to do anything but what they are told to do by the government. Look what happened to Chinese protestors in Tiananmen Square. Plus, the government is willing to rip off anybody's anything. Fuck intellectual property right. I thought their dominance would come about via a different pathway however.

In any case, look at the world right now. Though there is all kind of other things going on: there are all the interpersonal crisises, the political upheavals, the cries for change, and all that. But, all of them are/everything is now dominated by the fact that we are living through the first global pandemic provided to us by China. How fucked up is that? Why is nobody mad?

Whether COVID-19 was born in the wet markets of Wuhan or out of a Chinese bio weapons laboratory, as some have alleged, it doesn't even matter. What was created in China is dominating all of our lives. It is destroying many a life. Like a biologist I heard speaking on the news stated, *"The virus is feeding on us and using our bodies as its transport mechanism."* Why is no one pissed off and taking China to task?

"Love everything that exists in this moment and you will be free." If we look for the good in all

we are experiencing, there are a lot of lessons that can be learned and, I am certain, we have all encountered new levels of life existence that most of us never even thought that we would. If we control our thoughts, if we guide our emotions, we can come to love anywhere that we are.

So, you can love everything if you want—if you have the mental control to take control. Remember, that is all it is, mental control. Or you can let the goings on in the world or the emotions of your moment control you. Your choice. But remember, love everything that exists in this moment and you will be free.

Conspiracy Theory for the Day:

China has tested the perfect pathway for world dominance. They now know by releasing a virus they can destroy the economy of other countries and set the world into turmoil. All they have to do next time around is first develop a vaccine for the virus, give it to the their people, not give it to anyone else, and they win the game. Think about it…

*   *   *

12/Jun/2020 09:38 AM

The next time you are in a rush to get something completed that must be done think about all of the time you wasted doing nothing.

Lost and Gone Forever
12/Jun/2020 08:35 AM

If you paint a painting on a canvas it is probably going to last for quite a while. If you paint in on paper it won't last as long but it will probably be around for a while. You can make a lot of things last if you try. But, what about the things that do not last, the things that are here and then they are gone. …Things that you created and you really liked but they were lost to the winds of time way too soon?

I've never been a fan of theatre or theatrical acting. It's just not my generation. It's all too implied. But, there are a lot of people, particularly actors, who love it. They love the character and the audience interaction.

The thing about theatre is that it is here and then it is gone. Even if an actor is in their moment, even if they feel they really captured the essence of the character, it only lasts for that moment—here and then it is gone. And, once it's gone, there is no record left of its existence. Thus, what did that theatrical play actually equal?

This is the same with music—playing music live. Sometimes you and your band mates or the people you are playing with really get into this grove, it's like magic, you are all playing exactly what you should and some profound level of transcendence is achieved. It's here but then it's gone.

As a musician, I've experienced those moments. Afterwards all I could think about is that I wish we had recorded that session.

But, even when you record things sometimes they are lost. This is especially the case as technology has changed and the equipment of the past has been left by the wayside.

A couple of examples for me are, I used to have this Moog synthesizer and this Roland drum machine. Back in the days of analogue technology, you could run a cable and link the two together, and they would sync-up producing this incredible music. I would sit for hours creating great rhythm/synth music. Back then, recording was expensive. There weren't the relatively inexpensive home recording set ups that came along a bit later. So, at least in my case, all that music was lost. Though the perfection of that music is locked in my mind, no one else will ever hear it. So, what did my creating it actually equal?

In another case, a couple of years later, I had picked up the first generation of the Tascam 4-Track cassette recorder in Japan. This unit and its later incarnations came to rule the musical world in the 80s, giving musicians and bands an easy way to record their music.

Most people don't know this about me but I was very much into what was then titled Death Rock, which later became known as Goth. One night, sitting in my apartment, I recorded what I considered this great piece of music which really hit that early 80s Goth right on target. Time went on, life moved on, I moved on. In the early twenty-first century I came upon the tape that it was recorded on. Still owning a 4-Track cassette deck, I took it out and played the tape. It was still great. It was still right on, as I had remembered it. I rewound it to play it again but the tape was old and somewhere between the heads of the deck and the age of the tape it got destroyed. It was gone. Lost. This perfect guitar, bass, and drums recording lost forever. It did and it still does make me very sad that it is gone forever.

Think about creative situations in your own life. Think about the creations that you made that were important to you—that really meant something to you but somehow/someway now they are gone, they are lost. How did those creations define your life? What did they mean to you? What does it mean to you and your life that they are gone? How does losing them define where you find yourself in life right now?

For each of us, in our life, we create something. Some creations are very deliberate like art. Others are more abstract. But, whether your creation is painted on a canvas, doing your nine-to-five job just right, or being the best parent that you can be to your child, we all create something. The problem is, not all creations stand the test of time. Not all creations are appreciated or celebrated by other people. Some creations are just lost. Then what?

The thing about art is, the thing about creation is that everything in life holds little sense of permanence. We all want what we love to last forever. But, whether it is our favorite restaurant that goes out of business, the car that we loved that just got too old to keep on the road, or that painting that we painted and we really liked so we gave it to someone we cared about but they just threw it away, nothing last forever. Though most of us wish that was not the case, that is the reality of life. I know, that's no comfort. I know, there is no magical spell that will bring what once was back to life. But, that is the reality we all must live with.

So… When you are really in the moment with something… When you feel you have touched that perfection… When the paint is going on perfectly, the music is playing flawlessly, when you are in the perfect moment with that someone else, truly live it—live it like you may never feel it again. Because tomorrow it may all be gone and then all that will be left is only you holding onto the memory of what once was.

Looking for Someone to Hate
10/Jun/2020 04:10 PM

Especially on the internet, and all its various platforms, you can instantly witness a lot of people saying a lot of very bad things. You can call them, *"Trolls,"* as that seems to be the term commonly applied but by whatever name there are a lot of people saying a lot of very degrading things. They are attacking people for no reason other than their own distorted logic. And, they get away with it. That's not good.

As we have been thrust into this time period of rapid and radial change, due to the killing of a man at the hands (or should I say knee) of a police officer, things have begun to change very quickly and a lot of people have been targeted. I mean, long running television shows are being cancelled. The stars of TV series and Reality TV shows are being fired due to something that they once said that is now being deemed inappropriate. It's all pretty crazy.

But, what is taking place is so limited. The big players are the one's being focused upon but are the people who are out there saying bad things about people, telling lies about them, making derogatory statements about people, are they being focused upon? No. Their lies and distorted interpretations of a person's life is still available, especially on the internet. So, what is really changing? If you think about it, it is only the superficial representation of what is really going on and what is really going on is that at the root of human culture and at the heart of many a person's thinking ideology all they are about is judgment, whether that judgment be based in racist ideology or anything else.

Certainly, white people are in the bull eyes right now. And, a lot of them are out there, protesting in the streets, attempting to change how the world's people interpret their everything. But, white people are not the only people who are racist. As I have told the story way too many times, I grew up the only white kid in my grammar school and the level of black on white racism that was directed towards me on a daily basis was immense. But, my family had nothing to do with slavery or keeping anyone from becoming anything. My heritage goes back to Scotland. My family was not here during the time of slavery. My grandparents who came to America lived very humble lives. On my mother's side, my grandfather was a blacksmith and later a factory worker. On my father's side, his father worked for the railroad and his mother was a dental hygienist. So, why am I (or anyone like me) being blamed for the black condition?

When any of us meets another person, of course, we take note of their race. Just as if we see a blonde person or a redhead, a person dressed like a biker, a cowboy, or in a three-piece suit we take note of that fact. But, for most of us, that is not the final basis of our judgment. We deicide if we like the person, if we have anything in common with them, if we appreciate what they do or do not do, and how they encounter the world. From this, we decide if we want to hang out with them or not. This is the twenty-first century and a lot of people are still associating race as the primary culprit when that is rarely the case.

A lot of people have been out in the streets over the past two weeks. This has all been based upon what a cop did to a man—a man who was a convicted felon, who was on drugs, and who may have committed a crime. And, that's fine. As an artist I know sometimes inspiration comes from unexpected sources. If a man with that background can inspire change, that's great! His life served a great purpose! But, at the root of all this anger, all this pent-up frustration, all this acting-out, all this screaming for change, is the person. Look around you, how many people have you known who have said something bad, negative, or judgmental about another person and from this that other person's life was damaged. How many people have you known who have hurt someone via physicality, stealing from him or her, or doing anything else that may have hurt them and then they dismissed their responsibility of ever doing anything bad? I imagine you've done it too.

People always want to focus on something outside of themselves. They always want to place the blame somewhere else. But, the blame is with you—with what you have done. It is your fault. What are you going to do about it?

People can take to the streets. People can attack other people on the internet. People in a position of power can fire someone for them doing something that is now considered unthoughtful or inappropriate. But, that is all people doing something outside of themselves. That's easy. That's a cop out.

What are you going to do about you? What are you going to do about the people you have hurt? What are you going to do about the bad things that you have done? If you say you've done none, you are lying to yourself. And, what are you going to do about the people your friends have hurt?

The only true place for change is in you. It is you changing you. It is you fixing the damage you have created. It is you caring enough to care about the other person. Do you? If you don't then you are a bullshit person. Don't take to the street or to the internet proclaiming a need for change. Don't blame anyone else. Don't attack the actions of anyone else. If you don't fix what you have done, if you don't fix what the people you know have done, then you are responsible for all the pain that is going on in the world. Maybe you don't care. A lot of people don't. But, if you don't care think what that says about you.

It is you who can change everything. That change begins with you. First, fix what you have broken, fix the damage you have created, undo the hurt you have unleashed. Do that before you ever discuss how the world needs to change.

Broadcasting Their Greatness
10/Jun/2020 10:14 AM

As the martial arts took hold in the United States in the 1960s and 1970s, not only did a large number of martial arts organizations come and go by the wayside but also practitioners began to desire to receive accolade for their accomplishments. They wanted to be deemed, *"Something Good," "Something More."* From this, there came to be a large number of groups that inaugurated, Hall of Fames. This especially took hold in the 1990s when the internet came to rule the world.

These Hall of Fames awarded a martial artist a certificate that proclaimed their, *"Goodness."* In some cases, some of these organizations had big yearly dinner ceremonies that went hand-in-hand with these award galas.

The thing about these Hall of Fame ceremonies, that many people did not know, is that most of these organizations charged the recipient to receive their award. I always thought that was bit strange. If someone was good enough to be in the Hall of Fame shouldn't their accomplishment be enough to guarantee their placement?

Back in the days when there were a lot of Hall of Fames, back when I was writing a lot of martial art orientated articles and books, I cannot tell you how many of them contacted me and asked me to become one of their Hall of Fame recipients. But, as there was always a price tag involved, I turned all of them down. Moreover, I've just never been one of those people who seeks accolades. I'm mean, it's just a piece of paper. This is the same with rank in the martial arts. I have encountered so many people with sky-high rank but they were lacking in the rudimentary knowledge of what the martial arts is truly about. Yet, because they had a piece of paper they could claim all kinds of superiority.

The thing about these Hall of Fames, and their recipients, is that from that award they could claim accomplishment. Their bio, whether it be truthful or fabricated, was set to stone and all who wondered about the person could find it listed somewhere on some website. Thus, making them an established, *"Something."* …A Hall of Fame receiver.

In the martial arts, at least here in the western world, it seems there has always been these low level practitioners who want to attack the credibility of other practitioners. Why they do that is anybody's guess but it's just stupid. I've written about this problematic condition in the past. But, what these Hall of Fames gave people is this abstract proof of substance. They were that, *"Somebody,"* that they hoped to become. They were that, *"Something,"* that somebody else was not. I guess that's okay, if that's what you're looking for…

I think to the martial art instructors I've studied from. Many of them where, what I would consider, true first-generation masters of the Korean martial arts. But, most of them, no one ever heard about. They were never in any Hall of Fame. They were just really good teachers who worked out of a small martial art studio. Did they need to claim anything? Nope. They just taught the martial arts.

In some cases, they too came under fire from low-level practitioners who wanted to diminish their standing in the mind's of other people or steal their students by claiming they were nothing great. But, if anyone does that, if they speak in that fashion, that only demonstrates his or her limited level of understanding of the true martial arts. That illustrates that they are not a true practitioner.

What does this tell us about true accomplishment? I believe it let's us know that a person can never be defined by a certificate on the wall. Because most certificates you have to pay for. In the martial arts you also have to pay to take your test to be promoted. Again, I have always had a problem with this practice. Which is why I never charged my students anything for their rank promotion. If they were good enough, they were good enough.

Yeah, I know, that makes me a bad businessperson. But, to me, I never taught the martial arts as a business. In all the years I formally taught, I never made a dime.

The question you should ask yourself is why do you want what you want? Why do you want to be deemed that, *"Something?"* And, are you willing to pay for it? Plus, if you have to pay for it, what does that say about its validity?

So, the next time somebody tells you that they are a, *"Something,"* the next time someone proclaims they won a award—that they are in a Hall of Fame, ask them, *"How much did that award cost you?"*

* * *
10/Jun/2020 07:18 AM

Do you ever question why a specific thought comes into your mind?

A Time of Giving
09/Jun/2020 07:29 AM

Every now and then every culture reaches a time of change. This may be brought on by any number of factors but when this occurs it shakes the core of the civilization and it causes people to reevaluate the status quo.

Of course, there is always resistance to change. Some/many people despise change. They want everything to stay the way it was. But, once this culture shakeup is set into motion, the way things were have the potential for change.

I use the word, *"Potential,"* for a reason. Because that is truly all it is. There is the potential. There is no guarantee. If you look to the culture revolutions of the past, yes, there may have been a lot of belief that things were going to change and a new cultural landscape would emerge, but looking back most change was left only to the surface of a culture, true internal change did not take place.

Certainly, the U.S. has recently been thrust into a time of cultural upheaval. People have taken to the streets and politicians, playing the politician game, have been making promises. But, look across the globe, look throughout history; rarely has any of this behavior resulted in a major cultural shift. Yes, political parties may change. Yes, there may be a few new laws put on the books. But, at the root level of the society nothing is very different. In the hearts of the people, they are still the same.

Protests bring out opinions. Protests breeds mob mentality. Protests incite riots. Protests provoke demands. But, even if the demands are met, in small doses, does that change the root mentality of a culture?

Though people become aroused and even enflamed during the time of large-scale protests, what they do not do is find a way for themselves to personally give. Yes, they may be part of a group consciousness. Yes, the may be hoping for the same end-goal. But, all that is outside of the Self. All that is based upon somebody else doing something to give them what they want. It is not about them giving anything to anybody. Due to this mindset, the true essence for change is lost, in these times of upheaval, and that is why they eventually die down and little is truly accomplished.

What do you plan to give anybody today? Did you wake up with a game plan that was designed for you to do anything for anybody?

What do you want today? Did you wake up with a game plan that was designed to get you what you want?

If you think about this, if you study your own life, you will see that this is the common pattern of life. You want to get what you want. You may even be enraged and want your society to change. But, that is something that you want. You may even be willing to go outside and march, carry a sign, and yell and scream. But, that is all a drug. The drug of adrenaline.

At the heart of any society are the people. At the root of all peoples is the person. It is at this level, person-to-person, that a society is truly created. It is what one person does for the next person that defines the overall culture of a people.

Again, what do you plan to give anybody today? Did you wake up with a game plan that was designed for you to do anything for anybody—any one person?

If you want your society to be better, it must begin with you. It must begin with what you do. What are you going to do? What are you going to do for what and for whom? What are you going to give anybody today?

Stealin' When I Shoulda Been Buyin'
08/Jun/2020 09:40 AM

There are a couple of titles that I have used more than once, over the years, while writing this blog and this is one of them. There is the Uriah Heep song from 1973 called, *"Stealin',"* and the main lyric to this song is, *"Stealin' when I shoulda been buyin'."*

The reason I have come back to borrowing this title, more than a once, is that I see so much of this type of behavior going on and it is just wrong. There are all of the these people stealing all of this stuff and they are not even thinking about the person they are stealing from or what their stealing will do to that other person or persons; they are only thinking about themselves. From a moral perspective, I believe that we can all agree this behavior is selfish and wrong. But, how about you, how much stealin' do you do? Stealing goes on all around us, all the time.

Certainly, in the recent week, there was all of this looting taking place hand-in-hand with protests, leading to riots, that broke out across the U.S. Think how many lives were damaged due to that stealing. Did the people doing the stealing care? Does the stealer ever care?

This is not the first time in U.S. (and world) history that this style of radical protest has taken place. Out of the 1960s rose groups like Students for a Democratic Society, leading to the Weather Underground, the Yippie movement, guided by people like Abbie Hoffman and Jerry Rubin, onto the Black Panthers. Each of these groups took their left leaning ideologies to the extreme and were willing to hurt other people to gain their goals. Did they succeed? No, not really, because the protests of today are still fighting for the same ideals these groups of the past proclaimed. Sad but true.

Think about your own life. What have you stolen? Was it blatant stealing like forcefully taking something that was not yours? Was it passive stealing? Did you take something from someone else that they did not agree to give it to you? Or was it doing something like buying something, using it for a awhile: reading it, watching it, or listening to it and then returning it for a refund once you were done? That's stealing too.

Think about your own life, if you have stolen anything, were you considering how your stealing would affect the anyone else? Probably not. Most stealers never think about the other person, they only think about themselves and what they do or do not want.

If you have stolen and you have not thought about the other person, what does that say about you as a human being? What does that say about anyone who steals?

There is and has always been all of these things going on in the world that people don't like. As it is always the case, all of this like or dislike is based upon personal perspective. One person likes what another person hates and vise versa. Okay, that's life. That's reality. From this, periodically is born a reason to protest. Again, that's life, that's reality. But, what all life ultimately boils down to is personal action. What one person does to someone else. All life actions, be they seen as good or bad, positive or negative, are born with one person doing one thing. This is why the actions of one person leads to the reactions of someone/everyone else.

For example, look at what is going on right now, leading to all of this protest; one cop did one thing to one person. One person, (the cop), believed the other person to be committing a crime. He arrested him and from his unconscious actions he killed the man. Thus, we can see how the actions of one person can lead to complete global chaos.

This is the same for you. This is the same for the things that you decide to do. If you steal, no matter what your motivation, you have the potential to unleash a wave of anarchy. Though that may sound all kinds of rebellious and poetic it is not because in mayhem and lawlessness people get hurt. Does anybody deserve to be hurt? Do you?

So, here we are. People are stealing. It happens all the time. It seems that every thief is always able to come up with a reason to justify their stealing. They justify their actions but they never take the time to consider what their stealing is going to do to the anyone else. Is that right?

As life begins with you—as life begins with your actions, it is only you who can choose to take a pathway where you do the most that you can do to be sure that no one will be hurt. It all begins with small things. It all begins with you doing the right thing. It all begins with you considering the other person before you choose to act. It all begins with you not taking anything that is not yours.

You can steal, it's easy, a lot of people have. But, stealing always hurts someone, no matter what your motivation. If you support people who steal, you are condoning their actions; you are ignoring the person who will be hurt by their stealing. Is that right? Does anyone have the right to hurt anyone? Does anyone have the right to hurt you?

Think before you do. Think about the other person. If you perform this action the entire world becomes just a little bit better as far fewer people will be stolen from, thus fare fewer people will be hurt.

* * *
08/Jun/2020 07:46 AM

Think, if you got rid of all of the things you have that make noise how much quieter would the world would be?

* * *
07/Jun/2020 07:14 AM

Will all of the bad things you've done be erased when you die or will your actions live on?

Will all of the good things you've done be erased when you die or will your actions live on?

Take a Moment To Appreciate Where You Are
06/Jun/2020 07:35 AM

Most of life passes by in a flash. What you are living is here and then it is gone. For most, life is lived more via their memories than it is in the moment those memories were formed. They are so busy looking to the something else that what is going on is gone before it is realized that it was something worth truly living instead of something simply worth remembering.

All life is special. All life is worth the living.

Most people do not feel unless they are forced to truly feel. They only feel when they are engulfed in those moments of intense emotion. From this, they seek out those moments, they try to create those moments, for in those moments is the only time they feel alive.

Living your life in this fashion is a fool's elixir, however. It causes people to walk down all kinds of dark pathways in order to find that place where those heightened feelings are encompassed.

Again, all life is special. All life is worth the living. Each moment holds its own perfection, its own joy, and its own realizations.

Look at the moment you are living right now. Where are you? What are you experiencing? What are you feeling? Who are you with? What do you feel about them? What do they feel about you? Is this moment going to be remembered or are you simply killing time, waiting for something grander in which you can truly feel?

If you are constantly looking away from this moment/any moment, hoping to feel something else, all of your life moments will be lost. All of the perfection that exists in the mundane will never be experienced and you will only remember your life moments when you are encountering the most extreme levels of emotion. From this, most of your life will be lost. Most of what you could have felt, could have experienced, will never have been truly lived.

Take a moment right night: feel what you are feeling, experience what you are experiencing. Listen, and truly hear, look and truly see, feel and truly understanding.

Homework for the day…

Take today and truly take the time to experience your life. Come to know, come to see, come to feel all that there is to know, see, and feel. Wherever you find yourself, experience your experience. From this you will quickly come to understand that all life provides a plethora of enhanced, essential, and important feelings and experiences all worth feeling and experiencing, all you have to do is to open up and truly live them.

The Things That You Will Never Be Thanked For
05/Jun/2020 04:33 PM

I came home today and noticed a small package sitting on my mailbox. Looking at it, I realized that it was actually addressed to my next-door neighbor. The mail carrier that delivers to my area is fairly lackadaisical about her job. Though nice, she just doesn't really care and this kind of stuff happens all the time. So, I walked it over and put it on their mailbox. They will never know what I did. They will simply think that the package was properly delivered to their address. And, that's okay. I seek no thanks. I was happy to do it. I was glad that I could do it.

This is the thing about life. Think about it… So few people do anything unless they receive something in return for their actions. They want to be rewarded. They want to be thanked. How about you? What do you do for others expecting nothing in return?

There is a lot of turmoil in the world right now. We've got COVID-19 and we have all of these protest all across the U.S. that have, in some cases, spread across the world based upon a handcuffed man being killed by a police office with his knee on the man's neck. Sure, the guy might have committed a crime, but the issue is much bigger that that. He was a human being!

Many people have focused on the fact that the man was African-American. But, the issue is much bigger than that. It is the fact that people do all kinds of things to other people, no matter what their race, their gender, or their lifestyle, and they do it without thinking or caring about the damage that they are instigating. How about you? What do you do to other people without taking the time to consider that they too are a human being?

The thing is, we can all step in and help. We can all deliver the mail to the house next-door. We can all do something that helps someone. We can do it and nobody has to know that it was us doing the doing.

Think about it... How much time do you spend helping someone else who never knows that you are helping them? They can't thank you because they do not know that you did something good, positive, and helpful?

There is all kinds of negativity in this world. There are all kinds of people doing and saying bad things that hurt the life of other people. There are all kinds of people delivering a package to the wrong address because they do not care enough to do their job correctly. How much time do you spend helping to fix any of that?

There is life. There is strange abstract worlds like the internet. There is human-to-human contact. There is all kinds of stuff going on in the out there that you witness. How much in any of that do you try to help the person who is being hurt? How often do you try to help the person with a knee in their neck? How often when someone is saying something negative, which is just a painful as something physical, do you tell that person to stop it?

Now, I am not advocating helping the criminals: the rioters, the looter, the thieves, the rock throwers, the people painting graffiti on someone else's property, or the people stealing and ransacking the lives and the livelihood of the small business owners simply because they want what they have. What I am advocating is helping the person who needs help. The person who has been or is being hurt.

People place all kinds of definitions on why they are doing the wrong thing. Some do it with the, whoa is me mindset, others do it with a smile on their face. Most blame the other person. But, wrong is wrong is wrong. If what you are doing is designed to hurt someone, whether it is one person or a large group of people, the wrongness is obvious even if others revel in your accomplishments.

We can all make this world a better place. And, that better is not simply based in standing up for what we believe. It is about taking a stand against the bully, whether they have a badge or a loud mouth. We can help. We can try. We can only say or do positive things. We can help the person that will never know that we helped them.

So, what are you going to do next? Who are you going to help?

The Things That Never Happened
04/Jun/2020 04:35 PM

In everyone's life there is that something that you hoped would happen. Maybe it was winning the match, being with that girl or guy you liked, getting the job you really wanted, owning a beautiful house, a fast car, or being a movie star. For everyone, there is that dream that they dreamed but it did not happen.

Particularly when a person is young, the dreams are endless and if one thing doesn't turn out the way you hoped another dream takes over its place in your card catalogue of desires. The problem is, we all get old. We all are confronted with the realities of life. We all must find a way to make a living. And sometimes, the people we like do not like us. Reality takes hold and we all are forced to live an existence that was not all that we had hoped.

Though everyone seems to project that they very successful person is living the dream life, this is not always the case. I have known a couple of very successful people and they too experience feelings of not being completely satisfied and wishing certain things had turned out differently. So, it is everybody. It's not just you.

Some people really hold onto loss in their life. They really focus on what did not come to be. They continually reflect on the fact that their life is not what they had envisioned. In some cases, they even blame someone else for where they find themselves in life.

There are people who look back to the past and they remember that person who got away. In this day and age of easy contact and quick-find, some people attempt to reconnect with that distance relationship. A few people from my past have contacted with me and though it was great to hear from them and in a couple of cases re-met them, we were completely different people from who we were back then. What was then is not what is now.

I have this one friend who has been pretty alone for the last decade or two and he tried to reconnect with his high school girlfriend. I mean, that is pretty weak. She was married; had kids. Just because he was still solo does not mean that the other person had not moved on. The past is the past and it just makes you look bad to try to push your way back into a relationship lost long ago.

For me, I am not a very nostalgic person. There is none of those feelings of the, *"One who got away,"* or anything like that. Sure, I realize there were a couple of times when I turned right when I should have turned left. But, that's life. You have to live what you have to live.

All this being said, for many people there is that one thing that they really wanted. Maybe there is that person they wanted to be with or that thing that they hoped to become. What is it for you? Take a moment right now and really define that thing that you hoped would come into your life. Really think through this. Delve deep into the fantasy. Go back to the inception of that desire and really follow it through in your mind as if you had lived what you hoped you had lived. Really embrace it. Make it real.

A side not here: for those of you interested in Astral Projection or Time Travel this is the basic formal for those mental realms.

As you are following through that dream you wish you had lived, really look into the truth of that reality. Don't let yourself simply be bathed in absolute perfection, as nothing in life is like that. Really see the situation for what it is—see it for what it would have been. See where it would have lead your life and visualize some of the experiences you would have had.

If you are real with yourself, you will come to realize that there is a price to pay for everything in life. Every accomplishment, every relationship, every acquisition comes with a price tag. What would have been the true cost of you living your dream?

The reality in life is it is never everything that we had hoped—it is never exactly as we expected. From a philosophical perspective, we can all understand that to be truly happy, to be truly free, we must be accepting and thankful for the things that we have, even though they are not necessarily all that we wished for.

The main thing to keep in mind is that, yes, we all wish our life could be more, could have been more. We all want that something more. But, that is not what panned out. This is your reality, welcome to it.

This is not to say that you should not pursue your dreams. This is not to say that you should not try to become all you hope to become. But, always keep in mind that no matter what you accomplish, no matter what you achieve, it will never be exactly as you expected. Be real with yourself and know, no matter what you have you will always want something more.

* * *

04/Jun/2020 01:39 PM

In life you will find that those who judge you the harshest are generally the ones who should be judged the most harshly.

* * *
03/Jun/2020 04:27 PM

If you've hurt one person you've hurt one person too many.

What are you going to do about it?

I Came To Get Some Money
03/Jun/2020 07:37 AM

Virtually everyone who commits a crime has a reason for doing so. Maybe that reason is only in their own mind but nonetheless they have a reason. Maybe that reason will cause someone else to feel a lot of pain but nonetheless they have a reason for committing that crime. Maybe that reason is completely selfish, unthinking, and self-serving, but nonetheless they have a reason for committing that crime.

It is no secret that over the past week the U.S. has been blowing up with riots in many cities due to the death of a man held on the ground by a police officer's knee as he kept exclaiming, *"I can't breathe."* There's a lot of anger in the streets and on the minds of many. Rightly so. This has fed into protests for change, leading to riots.

There always needs to be impetuous for change. The sad fact is, riots and the people who participate in the destruction and looting that go hand-in-hand with riots, rarely have the expanding greater good on their minds. Sure, they may be motivated by what has taken place but destruction only equals destruction and stealing only equals loss, and crime (of any kind) only equals hurt.

Moreover, I would guess that a large percent of the people who are out there doing their crimes, in the midst of the riots, are not even registered to vote or cannot be registered to vote. So, how will what they are doing truly affect any positive change to take place?

Of course, all that is taking place has been well documented by news crews. There was a reporter the other night that went up to a young man who had been arrested for looting and he asked the man where he was from and why he had done what he had done. The young man was not from the Los Angeles area, he had traveled here specifically for the reason of committing a crime, and he exclaimed, *"I came here to get some money."* Meaning, he did not come here for the protest, he can here to rob and loot.

Does anyone ever think when they are committing a crime about how their crimes will hurt another person? Do they care? Probably not. As long as they get what they what, by whatever means possible, all they are thinking about is themselves. And, this is the problem with crime on any level.

Crime takes place all over the place. It happens all of the time. The problem with crime, and its many levels of existence, is that it is very common that the person who is committing the crime does not take the other person, who is on the other end of the crime, into consideration.

Here's a story for you… It is certainly not on the level of the crimes of looting businesses and life destruction that have been taking place but it goes to show you how even small crimes can come to affect an entire life and how all lives and the life of all people are weirdly intertwined.

Very early in my attendance at Hollywood High School I became fast friends with this other new student. He lived in Laurel Canyon next door to Frank Zappa and that was cool. But, mostly we got on very well. As we were both part of that longhaired, get high, counter culture crew of the early 1970s, we associated with those of our kind and we would go and smoke weed out on the school bleacher at lunch. I don't know where I was but my friend was out there getting high when a group of straight-laced guys came upon them. Most of our crew ran one way while my friend ran another. Those guys chased him, caught him, turned him in, the school called the police, he got arrested, and he got kicked out of school. (Remember this was the early 70s).

Time went on and I got to be friends with another guy. Though different from me, in terms of style and life focus, I thought him to be a nice guy. His father had rented him his own apartment and for someone in high school that was beyond cool. We hung out, got high at his apartment, went to concerts together, and the like. Months later, my original friend came to visit one day. High schools were pretty much open back then with no fences or gates so this was no big deal. Glad to see him and all that, he looks over to my new friend and told me that he was one of the guys who turned him in. Wow, what do you do with information like that? On one hand, my original friend was committing a crime, smoking dope. On the other hand, my new friend had committed a moral crime, turning him in. This, while he too got high.

We are all motivated by our circumstances and the people we associate with. In some cases, we choose a specific type of person to hang out with. In other cases, we have little choice. From all of these factors: family, culture, lifestyle, and friends we are driven to do the things that we do. But, in life there is always a choice. There is the choice to do the right thing and there is the choice to do the wrong thing. The only problem is, in some cases the line between these two becomes blurred. Why are they blurred? This is generally based upon interpersonal definition. What you want to do and what other people are suggesting that you do. From this, crime is committed.

If you watch the footage of all of the riots that are taking place it is obvious that some people are there for one specific reason, they want to target and rob a businesses. Some of these people are so stupid. Cameras are everywhere now and their faces are being filmed as they walk out of businesses with hands full of stolen items. Plus, some are being filmed loading things into their cars. You can see their license plates! I guess there have been tons of arrests over the past few days based on this footage but that did not stop the destruction and the looting. I am certain this looting, combined with the fact that so many businesses have being closed under COVID-19 pandemic lock down for the past two months, will destroy any chance of them reopening. People were hurt by these crimes! Did those criminals care or even know about what instigated any of this? Probably not. As stated by the one man, *"I came to get some money."*

Here we are. We are confronted by crime all the time: the small crimes people do to other people that changes their lives, the crimes the system does to people that may kill them, and the crimes people do to other people simply because they want what they have. How wrong is all that? How wrong are you? What motivates you to do what you do and do you ever think about or care how what you are doing will unleash a crime onto someone/anyone else?

* * *
01/Jun/2020 01:00 PM

There's a difference between a person who can't get up and a person who won't get up.

*　　*　　*
01/Jun/2020 07:31 AM

Most people feel no guilt about taking something from somebody. They only get upset if they are caught.

Kiss the Enemy
30/May/2020 07:29 AM

For each of us, I imagine that at some time in our life we have encountered someone that we do not really like. Generally, the reason we do not like a specific person is that they have done something to us or said something about us that has hurt our life. From this, we naturally feel anger. The problem with feeling and holding onto this anger is, however, the fact that those feeling are held mostly in our mind. We feel them. We amplify them. We think and rethink about them. But, all of this leads to nothing. Nothing more than a lot of negative emotions held in our own mind or possibly equally physical reaction. Okay… How about this… Instead of hating a person from afar or trying to get back at them why don't you put all the nonsense behind you and go up and give them a kiss?

Physically touching another person, in a positive manner, is one of the best, most healthy, and healing things that a person can do. It immediately changes the dynamic of any situation. Instead of hating, instead of elongating any negative anything, simply go up to a person and change the everything by giving them a positive kiss. Go make love.

Now, I get it, many times dislikes are held between two people of the same gender who are not drawn to that style of physical behavior. So, you don't want to go up and kiss a person of the same sex as that may completely inflame things. In those cases, the bridge to changing the dynamic of the relationship does not have to be so intimate. It can simply be a positive gesture like a handshake or a hug. The entire thing about this process is that one person needs to be the bigger person and make the effort in a stunning, direct, and positive manner, and from this everything changes.

Just for example, think about a person of the opposite sex you have had a beef with. Think if you went up, smiled, said a few kind words, and then kissed them. Think how everything would change.

I'm not saying anything here about forcing your physicality onto anyone. That's just wrong. But, the fact is, if you can break down the obstacles between the two of you, make true contact, you can come to have an entirely different understanding about a person and they about you. But, to do this, you have to be open enough to break down the barriers.

I do not believe that most of us wish to have conflict between us and any other person in our lives. Generally, the someone else caused the conflict, though many people are not unfamiliar with being the instigator. Whatever the case of inception, put all that on the back burner, make contact, be nice, say you're sorry if you're the instigator, tell the person you understand their feelings, and give them a kiss.

Kissing (or some other physically positive action) is one of the best alleviators of conflict. And, less conflict not only makes your life better but it make the whole world and the all and the everything just a little bit better.

The White on Black Screen Credits
29/May/2020 09:23 AM

If you've ever watched independent feature films from the 1980s and the 1990s, even break out hits like *Mad Max,* you will observe that most often the front end screen credits are commonly presented in white lettering over a black backdrop. There is no real artistic or scientific reason for this, it was done simply because that was the cheapest way to do it. In this day and age of digitally done everything, people often forget (or did not know) that in the filmmaking process everything hits your budget in different ways. For example, when we were finishing up *The Roller Blade Seven,* a company that was designed around doing screen credits (and there were many) would call me up several times a week trying to get me to use that company. The problem was, to get over-picture credits back then was not cheap. For RB7 it would have cost us about fifteen thousand dollars—money our post production budget didn't have.

Now, today, the indie film does virtually everything within the computer realm, of one sort or another. Because it has become very cheap, the cost of titling is generally not even placed in a film's budget anymore except for the time involved.

The reason I discuss this is due to the fact that back then an interesting/sketchy thing would sometimes happen to indie films that illustrates the reason why it was not the best of ideas to lay white credits on black. Think about it… Those credits were laid into the front end of a film which, except for the words, there was other no actual link to the film. Any title, any cast member, any crew member, could be in any film. You wouldn't know until you saw the film. Even then, if you didn't know, you didn't know.

What was not uncommon, in that era, was that some distribution company, generally in the Asian or Latin market, would get a copy of a film, change the title, completely alter or pull out the original front end screen credits and market the film without paying the producers anything. Who would know?

Back in the days when videotape was king, there were video rental and retail stores all over the globe. Each offered products for the local viewing audience to consume. As these stores required a constantly evolving line of products, they were always seeking out new titles. Grab a movie from somewhere, change the title, pull out or change the cast and crew credits, and these distributors were good to go. They could make money and pay nothing.

As someone who has spent a lot of time in Asia, there were a couple of time when I would be wandering around a video store and find one of my films being offered by a distributor that I had not made any deal with. The title would be something different. The only thing that pointed me to the film was the video box photo. I still have a couple of those videotapes somewhere.

To the average person, who cares? They're just watching a movie. To the filmmaking, well that's a different story.

I guess this all goes to the philosophic debate about creation. There is the creator, the person or persons who imagined the idea and then brought that idea to life. Then, they put it out there for the world to see. Who owns it? The creator or the people who view it?

Sure, sure, we can go down the road of business and all that... From that perspective, stealing the something the someone created is always wrong. People should not be allowed to make money while the creator is not paid. But, from the perspective of art, once it is out there it kind of becomes everybody's. Isn't that what the creator hoped for? ...For his (or her) art to be viewed by as many people as possible. I guess it comes down to the debate of getting credit were credit it due.

From the perspective of an artist, I've always signed my paintings on the back. I find/believe that the piece of art should be whole and complete onto itself. Thus, I do not want my signature to distract from the actual work of art. I get it, if it's a famous artist, the whole reason you want their signature on the front of the canvas is so you can say, *"Look whose art I own."* But, that is a whole other genre.

But, more to the point, when you watch a film—when you read the credits, how do you truly know who did what? How do you know that what is presented on that screen is the actual person? In fact, in life how do you know who did what? Do you simply believe the name associated with the whatever simply because it is up there on the screen for you to see?

Life is a complex interplay of creative forces. There are those who create. There are those who have the vision and the inspiration. There are those who bring things to life. There are also those who hope to make money off of what others create. There are those who steal. They steal what they steal for whatever reason but they have stolen nonetheless. Once they have stolen some try to alter the truth of the creation and the creator's creative process without giving them their due: financial or otherwise.

Ask yourself, do you believe the front end credits (of anything) simply because they are on the screen? Do you ever question the truth about what is being presented to you? If you don't, consider how easy it is to change that presentation. Contemplate how easy it is for someone, who had nothing to do with the creation, to modify the actual creator's truth about who did what and why. Though the true truth of the creation never changes in the illuminated spectrum of absolute reality, who gets credit and why is forever simply a word placed upon the screen; white on black.

Blame Where Blame is Due
27/May/2020 09:45 AM

I imagine that most of us have had the experience where we were asked to do something by someone and when they did not like the results they blamed us even though it was they who wanted us to do that something that we had no desire to do in the first place. Most commonly, in these situations, we are given, at best, some marginal instructions, sent out to do the do with no help from the person who actually wanted the doing done. They did nothing, they only did the commanding. Yet, when what was presented did not meet their expectations, they blamed us.

Certainly, this type of behavior goes on all the time in the work place but it also takes place all over life.

All of this behavior is based upon what is conceived in a person's mind. But, the problem always has been, what is envisioned in a person's mind, is illustrated in its perfect state. Therefore, when something is brought to life, particularly when it is produced by some other individual, the perfect version of the what is in an individual's mind is lost. But, is that the fault of the someone else? No. It is the fault of the person who had the vision and desired the outcome.

I have seen this so many times in the film industry where filmmakers have massive fits when what they had envisioned for a scene is not being orchestrated as had been anticipated in their mind. I have also seen this in regard to very small life things in life. I remember when I was a Boy Scout and working on a merit badge. My friend and I were told by the Scoutmaster to create the dinner and breakfast for one of our overnight hiking trips. We had no guidance whatsoever. Plus, we were like twelve years old and had to pay for all the food ourselves. Anyway, we got to the campsite and after preparing dinner, the Scoutmaster freaked out, completely yelling at us that he didn't like our menu. We were kids! We had no guidance or menu approval. He was the adult. Yet, he blamed us. Who's fault was that?

Even in spiritual circles I have witnessed it. Back in my days with Swami Satchidananda's Integral Yoga Institute there was frequently the, *"Swami,"* power plays unleashed by the advanced disciples. At one point I was asked to go and put up posters for an upcoming lecture in Venice. First of all, this is illegal. But, I did what I was asked to do. I drove around Venice stapling posters to telephone poles and places like that. I don't know if it was that the poster was too nice or what, but they were all quickly pulled down and not too many people attended the lecture. The Swami who sent me on the mission tried to blame me that I had not done my job. Why didn't you go and do it?

And, this is the thing… In life, people want things to be the way they want thing to be. If they are in a position of authority, they want people to do their dirty work to make what they want happen. Then, if they are not satisfied, they blame that other person or persons. But, what is missing from the blame is the fact that they did nothing in doing that whatever's implementation.

In fact, a lot of people pass through their entire life behaving in this fashion. From this, though they live frustrated and unfilled lives, they can live it while blaming others for their unhappiness and lack of fulfillment. How about you? Do you do this? Have you had it done to you?

In your life, you have your desires. In your life, you want what you want and you want it to be presented via the idealized image that you possess in your mind. How do you feel when that does not happen? How do you feel when what someone has done did not materialize in the way you wanted it to happen? How do you react when you are not receiving what you want?

How you live your life, how you do the things you do, comes to be the definition of your life. How you react to others, comes to be how you are defined in the mind of others.

How do you act towards others? How have you behaved towards others? Who do you ask to do what and why?

Most of us can point to times in our life when we have been forced to deal with the unrealistic expectations of other people. Maybe we were even blamed for them not being satisfied with what they asked us to do. All the being the case, it is only how we personally deal with other people, how we act and react towards other people, that defines the reality that we encounter in life and how we will be remembered.

Who do you ask to do what? Why do you ask them to do it? What do you expect their results to be? And, why won't you—why can't you do it yourself?

THE ZEN